COPING WITH DEATH
AND DYING

COPING WITH DEATH AND DYING

An Interdisciplinary Approach

Edited by

John T. Chirban

**UNIVERSITY
PRESS OF
AMERICA**

LANHAM • NEW YORK • LONDON

University Press of America,® Inc.

4720 Boston Way
Lanham, MD 20706

3 Henrietta Street
London WC2E 8LU England

Library of Congress Cataloging in Publication Data
Main entry under title:

Coping with death and dying.

Includes bibliographical references.
1. Death—Congresses. 2. Death—Psychological
aspects—Congresses. 3. Death—Religious aspects—
Congresses. 4. Terminal care—Congresses. I. Chirban,
John T.
HQ1073.C67 1985   306.9   85-20280
ISBN 0-8191-4984-5 (alk. paper)
ISBN 0-8191-4985-3 (pbk. : alk. paper)

This book is dedicated to all those who believe that they are always learning and try to understand views that are different from their own.

Preface

Over the past two decades helping professionals and non-professionals alike have reaped the benefits of publications and media attention which have sought to acknowledge the importance of death as part of the life cycle. Albeit that death is equated with a great deal of "mystery," much which is known has not been communicated. And even that which has been shared has often not been integrated in a proper context for the professional and the lay person alike.

This book emphasizes the necessity for such an interdisciplinary effort in assisting individuals in the process of the dying experience. It presents understandings by specialists in medicine, psychology and religion as they relate their individual and collective approaches for helping people cope with death and the professionals' interest for relating with others in serving the dying person.

There is no pretense here which suggests that this volume provides definitive answers about death and dying. But, as the product of a national interdisciplinary symposium, this book informs its readers about the essential processes in coping with death and dying and also seeks to reflect upon how medicine, psychology and religion can work together to assist individuals who are confronted with death and dying.

The single thread which runs through the medical, psychological, and theological presentations of the speakers is their emphasis upon the importance of "effective communication." The experts who share their thoughts in the following pages explain how their particular fields of specialization may assist in meaningful communication for the individual who encounters death. In the final analysis, it is suggested that human needs are best served and a comprehensive understanding concerning death is most available to all when those concerned are able to appreciate the varied perspectives and approaches that converge at the death experience. The remarks of the contributors to this publication result in an appreciation of death and dying as a complex topic, but one which illustrates how an open and receptive approach provides an understanding to the whole person. Finally, it is important to note that this book expresses professional sensitivity to the whole person in a serious yet highly readable way—as the chapters of this book are re-presentations of the symposium lectures.

I wish to express my deep respect and sincere appreciation to the presentors who reviewed the edited verbatims of their talks and my special gratitude to the Reverend Dr. Nomikos Vaporis, Eleni Baker, and Patricia Vaporis who made this second edition of this book possible.

John T. Chirban
Cambridge, Massachusetts

Contributors

Dr. John Chirban is Chairman of the Department of Human Development and Director of the Office of Counseling and Guidance at Hellenic College and Holy Cross School of Theology. In addition, he serves as an Associate Professor in Human Development at Harvard University and maintains a private practice in psychotherapy in Cambridge, Massachusetts.

Dr. Mel Krant is a former Professor of Medicine and Psychology at the University of Massachusetts Medical School. He is currently the Director of the Pain Clinic at Deaconness Hospital in Boston and serves as a physician in private practice of internal medicine.

Dr. Gerald Koocher is the Director of Training in Psychology at Children's Hospital and the Judge Baker Counseling Center. He is an Associate Professor of Psychology at Harvard Medical School and has served as Director of Research for the study of long-term child survivors of cancer.

Rabbi Earl Grollman is a pioneer in the field of pastoral counseling, crises intervention and thanatology. A Rabbi at Beth El Temple Center in Belmont, Massachusetts, he has written numerous books and has appeared frequently on television talk programs.

The Rev. Thomas Hopko is Associate Professor of Dogmatic Theology at St. Vladimir's Orthodox Theological Seminary and serves as pastor of St. Gregory the Theologian Orthodox Church in New York.

Peter Poulos is a Hospital Chaplain. He serves as Director of Training in Pastoral Care and Clinical Pastoral Education Supervisor at Methodist Hospital, Brooklyn, New York and maintains a private practice as a clinical social worker.

Dr. Herbert Benson is Associate Professor of Behavioral Medicine at Harvard Medical School. He is a cardiologist serving as Director of the Division of Behavioral Medicine and the Hypertension Section at Beth Israel Hospital in Brookline, Massachusetts. He is author of the best sellers *The Relaxation Response* and *Body and Mind*.

CONTENTS

Chapter One

THE DIALOGUE IN MEDICINE, PSYCHOLOGY, AND RELIGION

John T. Chirban

Mental health workers and the clergy have long been grouped together as "helping professionals." But does much of a relationship exist between them? Are their services similar? For example, should one go to a physician, to a psychologist or to a priest while in the turmoil of sorting his or her feelings in the face of death? Would the advice of these different professionals lead diametrically to opposed perspectives? Or would their differences be insignificant?

My task is to discuss the problems for the disciplines of medicine, psychology and religion as they might come together in serving the needs of one who is dying. I will summarily address methodological questions: What are basic similarities and differences between medicine, and psychology and religion? Can there really be dialogue among these disciplines? And, if so, how can dialogue occur?

The apprehension and even enmity between these fields is common knowledge. Actually, the disciplines have rarely shared peace or understanding. An article in last month's *Boston Globe* reflects the tension. There "the fact" was set forth that psychiatrists experience the subject of religion as "taboo in therapy" since "people perceive psychiatrists . . . in competition with the clergy."

Well, are they? To be honest, I feel much trepidation as I address an audience with mixed and possibly competitive backgrounds: students, teachers; laymen, clergy; patients, doctors, theologians, psychologists/psychiatrists; churched, unchurched.

Can such diversified groups really hear one another? Before considering this question, let's think about how mental health and religious professionals have understood one another. To do this, I

1

will provide a brief summary of what professionals in these fields have said about the relationship between science and religion. For the purpose of clarity I will distinguish between science and religion rather than attempting to sort out the various aspects—similarities and differences—in the disciplines of medicine, psychology and religion.

I. WHAT HAS BEEN SAID ABOUT SCIENCE AND RELIGION

As I have examined the literature concerning the dialogue between science and religion, the single fact that impressed me was that although many things have been said—the discussions often seemed fragmented, partial or diffused. For example, there is a considerable amount of writing about the "differences of science and religion."

A. THE DIFFERENCES OF PSYCHOLOGY AND RELIGION

It is not uncommon to read about general similarities of and differences between science and religion. After reviewing many of the studies, I deduced the following matrix which accounts for the various reviews:

	SCIENCE	*RELIGION*
1. FOUNDATION	Scientific	Theological
2. PHILOSOPHY	Anthropocentric	Theocentric
3. SPIRIT	Secular	Sacred
4. APPROACH	Self-Correcting	Dogmatic
5. ATTITUDE	Dispassionate	Committed

Although there are elements of truth to these characterizations, in addition to polarizing the fields and churning emotional and often defensive reactions from the professionals themselves, after serious examination, I believe such generalizations do not seem helpful. And, in fact, there are significant problems with these claims. For example:

1. Regarding the Claim that Science and Religion Have, Respectively, Scientific or Theological Foundations:

To state that it is solely science which uses the scientific method blurs our awareness of the fact that there are implicit "theologies" or assumptions about the nature of the person behind all personality theories. Certainly "objective" science itself professes an inherent philosophy. Also, to characterize religion as having only theological foundations is to forget that religion is shaped by methods of human beings; on the one hand, including the strengths of the scientific method, and, on the other hand, reflecting the interpretations of the individual theologian."

2. Regarding the Claim that Science and Religion Have, Respectively, Anthropocentric or Theocentric Perspectives:

To generalize about anthropocentric and theocentric qualities of science and religion is to suggest that science and religion present two distinct perspectives rather than to acknowledge the fact that science and religion are independently very broad fields with at least as many opposing as complimentary positions within each area. Furthermore, within each discipline one may identify approaches that are more or less anthropocentric or theocentric.

3. Regarding the Claim that Science and Religion are, Respectively, Secular or Sacred:

To polarize science and religion as secular versus sacred is to obscure and to collapse the reality that both fields reflect human and divine experience and workings. And although science may be presented as overtly descriptive and theology as clearly prescriptive, a closer examination of the fields evidences, at minimum, the inherent prescriptions in science and implicit descriptions of theology.

4. Regarding the Claim that Science and Religion Are, Respectively, Self-Correcting or Dogmatic:

To perceive science as self-correcting and religion as dogmatic reflects a lack of historical perspective. In the case of religion, the history of the Church demonstrates accomodation and changes in the presentation of the Message of the times. And, in the case of science, to perceive the field as basically self-correcting ignores the reality that numerous stubborn, dogmatic positions determine, in fact, what the schools of science are all about.

5. Regarding the Claim that Science and Religion Are, Respectively, Dispassionate or Committed:

It has been common to sterotype that scientists emphasize a distant, clinical approach to life and that theologians express a personal, caring approach in their work. Although these characterizations may, to some degree, be accurate, the fact is that when they become predominate styles they skew the power of the disclplines themselves. When science and theology, however, balance both a committed and dispassionate approach they are most effective.

In the final analysis, such generalizations have resulted in creating significant gaps but these statements have not offered clarification about the similarities and differences nor a constructive understanding

about the relationship between science and religion. Then, what of
the dialogue? Can we not offer any more information about the distinction between perspectives in these fields of inquiry? Let us consider what clinical and mental health professionals themselves say:

B. SURVEY OF PROFESSIONALS IN MEDICINE, PSYCHOLOGY, AND RELIGION

A recent article in a Boston newspaper reported the results of
an informal survey of area physicians, psychologists and clergy about
their interfacing roles. Findings revealed these diverse impressions:

1. From the Scientific Perspective

It was stated that many pastors were thought to be ill-prepared
to deal with anything more than "a nagging spiritual crisis." One
psychologist said, " . . . clergy do not distinguish someone who is
suffering from a psychotic depression over and against a simple disappointment."

But the range of views differed even within the disciplines. Psycho-
therapists evaluated the skills of clergy from: "It's sort of like people who talk to their hairdresser" to " . . . it is nothing less than the
clergy's sworn duty to tinker with the parishioners' emotional ail-
ments." One psychologist humbly stated, "There's a tendency among
psychiatrists and psychologists to exaggerate in an extreme way the
amount of skills they have. They often overrrate their effectiveness and
underate the effectiveness and intelligence of other professionals."

2. From the Religious Perspective

A clergywoman stated that the non-clinical relationship between
minister and parishioner is compatible with the counseling process
but can preclude the "I'm nuts" stigma often identified with therapy.
She said, "I can help a lot of people who feel talking to me is not
threatening, but the idea of a shrink is devastating." On the other
hand, one clergyman pointed out the need for the religious to be
clearly differentiated from the therapists as "complications arise because clergy may enter conflicting roles."

Therefore, we see that a dialogue between medicine, psychology
and religion often does not occur between these distinct positions.
The interface between science and religion seems to have unclear
boundaries, to be ill defined and to be emotionally charged—
involving territoriality, biases and a variety of ways of thinking about
the disciplines. So, is there a way to bring order over the confusion?
Can there really be a dialogue?

II. MODELS FOR A DIALOGUE

As I sorted through the literature, I thought that the most heuristic approach in trying to understand the relationship between these disciplines is to examine *how people think* about medicine, psychology and religion. Since we are concerned with bridging communications between medicine, psychology and religion, I thought it would be helpful to try to identify ways in which we think about these fields—that is, how we conceptualize the discussion—to clarify the structure of our thought. So, I will describe stages here, not as in a formal theory of structural developmental thought, but as approaches that I have witnessed and experienced in my interdiciplinary studies.

I will briefly introduce the stages of these models, and I will provide examples of scientists, psychologists and theologians who reflect the characterizations of the models. This presentation does not intend to identify all the possible models but seeks to make the point that there are different ways that people think about science and religion. I would like to suggests that effective communication between the disciplines will be facilitated to the degree to which people become clear about their own thinking and as they engage in the dialogue—as well as become open to the approaches of others.

Although medicine, psychology and religion are represented in the following discussions as units, I want to acknowledge, again, that these fields separately include a variety of perspectives, often conflicting with one another. In the diagrams of stages the solid circle represents the issue or phenomenon under discussion; e.g., a person who is coping with death. The vertical line is the direction of analysis; the "E" ('Επιστήμη) indicates a scientific evaluation; the "Θ" (Θρησκεία) indicates a religious evaluation; the "A" ('Αλή-θεια) represents Truth. In order to emphasize the major interest or to identify stages of thinking, I will distinguish rather than detail the discussion of medicine, psychology and religion. Examples from both disciplines of medicine and psycology will characterize the scientific perspective.

III. TERMS

In this discussion, science ('Επιστήμη) is defined as approaches which apply the modern scientific method. Religion refers to the specific system of faith of the individual (Θρησκεία). "Θρησκεία" (religion) rather than "theology" (Θεολογία) is translated here from the Greek. I reserve the term theology as "the experience of God," and, in so doing, understand that it may occur even outside of religion. "Theology" is discussed in the last model. Truth ('Aλή-θεια), here, refers to the Ultimate Truth.

As we review the following nine models of dialogue, you might ask yourself which paradigm best characterizes your approach to the interdisciplinary discussion. Also, consider whether or not you have observed the other perspectives. Most important, ask yourself if the style which you employ in your thinking is in your interest and how adequately it serves your intents.

As we review these models, I will reflect concerning how I have witnessed these approaches in my life, and I will provide examples of theorists whose works demonstrate the basic thrusts of these perspectives.

1. *Monolithic Model*

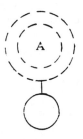

The monolithic model may reflect either a scientific or religious understanding. One of the distinctive features of the perspective is that it is basically egocentric. The egocentricity is experienced by how one is either uninformed or totally indifferent to views other than his own. From this model it seems that all of life can be interpreted according to either a scientific or theological vision. Material not made immediately clear through this particular approach is left unattended. This view is like that of a young child who sees only through his own eyes.

This perspective, however, may be represented by scientists or theologians who fail to take seriously the role of the "other" disciplines in life. Such individuals fail to acknowledge the existence of other perspectives and seem to need to explain all of life from their own vantage point. This results in a myopic and imperialistic approach.

2. *Beclouded Model*

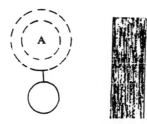

This model differs from the earlier conceptual framework in that it acknowledges that there are other perspectives. The individual, in this case, however, does not clearly understand what is "out there." This way of thinking is represented by those who know that there are perspectives about life different than their own but who are not clear about the details of the differences—neither what they are nor what they say—much less the way in which the "other" perspective interacts with the particular individual's perception of a phenomenon.

This may be demostrated by the physician in the hospital who is caring for the dying patient. Although he may acknowledge the chaplain as a member of "the team," he does not perceive the chaplain in terms which involve him or her nor does the physician make any attempt to clarify the uncertainty. The chaplain, in such an instance, may seem like an extra appendage.

Whether the physician, psychologists or clergyperson demonstrates this perspective, the point is that the other discipline seems to be a "clouded mystery." For all practical purposes, it is undifferentiated and outside of this person's immediate environment and needs and/or functions.

3. *Polarized Model*

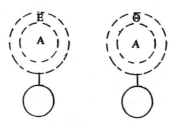

The polarized model clearly acknowledges and presents science and religion as being concerned with opposing or diffferent types of phenomena. The polarization is between their approaches—much like the distinctions that I identified in the earlier discussion of similarities and differences: Scientific vs. Theological; Anthropocentric vs. Theocentric; Secular vs. Sacred, etc. Here, psychology, for example, may acknowledge religion as identifying a certain reality but may treat it as a learned set of behaviors; and religion may acknowledge psychology as a useful discipline but may relegate its role to treating the "fallen nature of humanity."

After my first course in high school psychology, in retrospect, I saw that the polarization model seemed to provide me with a helpful way of managing what seemed to be my two different approaches to understanding life. This way of thinking provided me with a way to categorize and even to sterotype the functions of the disciplines for me. It enabled me to acknowledge conveniently the importance of psychology and religion as well as providing a method of avoiding the more complex aspects of life which were "gray" by placing them in this "either/or" matrix.

In college psychology, however, the polarization model did not seem to accomodate adequately my new concerns. At that time, I was introduced to behaviorism. In a sense, I found that the position of B. F. Skinner, with his presuppositions of determinism and "no choice," could not be rectified honestly by the limits of the polarization model. More specifically, the philosophical issues that Skinner raised could not be contained in the scientific part of the model.

And this created much tension and unrest within me. What to do with dissonance? Well, I approached my priest for his thoughts. After much discussion, he suggested that I read Skinner's work directly and that we should talk further. He wisely perceived that this was a growing edge for me. That summer, I worked in the mornings as a security guard, in Chicago. And with a gun that I really did not know how to shoot in one hand, and with one of Skinner's books in the other hand, I intensely read through the pages yearning to rectify my confusion. I prepared detailed notes from my readings and talked about the conflicting issues with my priest in phone conversations to Boston which would take place during the night.

After many conversations I finally mustered the nerve to pose my burning, bottom-line question. "So," I asked, "what if Skinner is right? What if there is 'no choice?' " To this he calmly answered, "If Skinner is right then religion is poetry." "But," he added, "the issue remains whether or not he is correct. This is something that you will have to decide for yourself.'' And so we move to the next model.

4. *Reductionist Model*

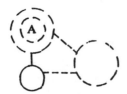

The reductionistic model dilutes the ''other'' position through prejudicial evaluations and a lack of serious attentiveness to the other's perspective. Functionally, this position maintains that the Truth is available only to its own constituency. Both science and religion have been guilty of this approach which is, in large measure, the reason for the tension that exists between them. Two cases in point:

Although it would not be accurate to characterize Sigmund Freud and B. F. Skinner in this way in every detail, nevertheless, they have done much to fuel psychological reductionistic perspectives. For Freud, religious practice and belief is prompted essentially by neurotic and psychotic motivation. He speak specifically of religion in terms of obsessive and compulsive traits, illusion and delusion; wish fulfillment and unresolved Oedipal striving; the return of repressed guilt and ''infantile patterns of helplessness''—in addition to projection and displacement.

And, for Skinner, religion is discussed and understood basically as a ''mode of control.'' For him, the teachings about heaven and hell epitomize the use of positive and negative reinforcement. Heaven and hell, he states, provide the foundation of religious power.

Most of us would agree that ''religious activity,'' in particular instances, may exhibit traits of these analyses, but we would not present these perspectives exclusively as representing the motives or functions of religion. In both instances, here, the psychoanalytic and behavioristic perspectives clearly reduce the intrinsic aspects of religion.

During my graduate work, I had the opportunity to discuss these concerns with B. F. Skinner, in terms of what I call here a ''psychological reductionistic approach'' between psychology and religion.

In that discussion, Skinner explained the purpose of religion as he saw it: "I would like to see religion permit one to examine the world, study it scientifically, without any threat that one is going counter to revealed truth. My own belief about God is that we are on a very small planet around a mediocre sun, which is one of billions of suns in our own galaxy and there are billions of galaxies. Now if God created all of that, who the devil are we to know anything about Him? I think it's ridiculous to suppose we can know God, and I don't see why God should reveal anything to us."

From this statement, it was evident to me that Skinner maintains an epistemology which precludes the experience of God. So I asked him, "Can there be other ways of being religious and experiencing God that are not explained through power and control—but through prayer? To this he responded, "Well, if God revealed Himself to us in the many different ways reported by different religions, and if I choose one, I would obviously choose one because of my culture, my own history." In saying this, the limits of Skinner's approach to the dialogue of science and religion are clearly drawn.

It should be noted that this same model may be witnessed inversely by the religious reductionistic perspective. Theologians who represent this approach may express defensive positions and/or sweeping generalities about medicine and psychology. In this model, they envision the Truth as accessible to religion alone and relegate the scientific disciplines to being faithless, secular and unnecessary. In addition to ignoring the fact that inspired, positive roles of religion have been affirmed by persons such as Jung, James and Einstein, the individuals represented in this model express a narrow, possessive attitude which suggests that they have the final hold on the Truth. They see little importance in work outside of their own sphere and they are closed to the truth that is available to other perspectives.

Whether the reductionistic model is maintained by science or religion, this approach purports to be all pervasive and comprehensive. Needless to say, it precludes an interactive, investigative or collegial dialogue.

5. Corrective Model

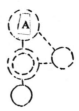

The corrective model attends to the value of the "other" perspective but has primary commitment to its own purposes. From the diagram, we may describe the discipline that is in line vertically (with a double dotted circle) as the *primary* discipline (whether medicine, psychology or religion) and the dotted circle to the right as the secondary discipline.

When religion is in the vertical position, the primary analysis is theological. Additional insights from the scientific community are heard—but, finally, a religious evaluation carries the authoritative weight. In this case, the bent or bias of this perspective inevitably concludes that religion provides the more penetrating analysis of the two approaches.

One may witness this model in pastoral psychological literature. This does not have to be the case, but writers in pastoral psychology, who work in this way, do not often describe their purposes which, in the final analysis, bring the religious perspective to the limelight. This approach is also documented by mental health professionals who do not understand religion. Although they may discuss faith, their primary allegiance is to a psychological evaluation.

One observes that in this model the particular discipline—not the dialogue—becomes primary. Usually, the secondary discipline is analyzed in the interest of the primary discipline. In doing this, obviously the secondary discipline is presented as having less importance.

Although somewhat dialogical, the model clearly reflects a one-upmanship: there appear to be vested interests by the "promoters" of this model and a need for their "primary discipline" to reign.

6. *Dialogical Model*

The dialogical model attempts to open a fair communication between science and religion. It affirms the inherent value in both science and religion and seeks to facilitate communication between these perspectives as they attend to human situations.

Like the polarized model, however, there often remains the perception that science focuses upon pathology while religion upon moral health. However, another, more critical problem is that this model, as presented by scientists or theologians, tends to overlook or to neglect the particular, implicit, methodological problems or unique contributions offered by science and by religion. In the effort to encourage the dialogue, therefore, important discriminations are not made. The boundaries of the disciplines are taken lightly or they are not discussed.

Efforts like those of Ernest Becker, *On Denial of Death,* or John Kornarakes, *On the Orthodox Tradition and Modern Psychology,* are cases in point. Although enlightening, these works do not give adequate attention their methodology and the commitments on which they are based.

7. *Theoretical Model*

The theoretical model is offered as "a goal" by people who speak about the values for interdisciplinary work between science and religion. This model is less than an approach to the dialogue as it tends to lack discussions of concrete phenomena. It is theoretical but not empirical. It represents more an *abstract* enterprise than a substantive dialogue through affirming the *principles* of a genuine dialogue between science and religion.

Elhard's work is illustrative of this approach, where features of what he calls "pervasiveness, relationship, tension, charge, identification and diffusion" are presented as structures in common between psychology and religion. The different theoeretical language, however, fails to be related to actual situations or concrete pheneomena.

The theoretical model works to consider seriously the aspects of a dialogue for science and religion. It is concerned with the methodological details and specific problems of each discipline. The discussion, however, is by theoretical abstraction and obviates the needs to consider both real situations and meaningful dialogues.

8. *Dynamic Model*

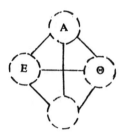

The dynamic model is concerned with the boundaries, methods and tasks of science and religion, and it attends to their content and to their implication as they relate to the phenomemon, e.g., the death of a child.

This model identifies the Truth as accessible to various disciplines as well as to the individual, i.e., in this case, the child. This approach to thinking maintains that no discipline has control upon the Truth. It emphasizes the strengths of the disciplines and engages one in a genuine dialogue in the full range of the resources. Differences are noted, not hidden. The resonant qualities of the disciplines are presented and affirmed. The dynamic model encourages a critical, serious relationship between medicine, psychology and religion.

An example of this constructive effort is noted in the work of James Fowler. Fowler's paradigm of faith development uses extensively the methods of various contributions from developmental psychology—including biological growth (Piaget) and moral development (Kohlberg) in the paradigm with additional sensitivity and careful attention to one's growth in dimensions of faith.

The dynamic model shows that the solutions to problems need not be understood from one or the other approches alone but that all fields, ideally, may draw upon each other's resources. Of what has been presented, it is the most balanced and objective approach to the dialogue—yet it demonstrating "desk-chair" qualities, being puristic, clinical, intellectual and idealistic. It does not seem adequately to present the *individual* in dialogue.

9. *Enlightened Model*

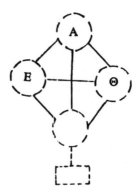

The enlightened model embraces all of the interests of the dynamic model with one very special addition: it resonates out of the beliefs and experiences of the individual who employs it.

This model not only offers maximal insight toward understanding a particular phenomenon, but it incorporates the individual, who takes ownership of his or her beliefs, biases and assumptions. It requires that one be clear in one's encounter of Truth, stating what are his or her convictions, or at least to own one's own vision—with the range of strengths and weaknesses that that implies. This model requires that one is grounded in a sense of self, having a foundation of self-awareness, in communicating in the interdisciplinary dialogue.

I find that the enlightened model most adequately incorporates the notion of theology as the "experience of God" to be distinguished from the discipline of theological discourse or religion, i.e., institutional activity which may or may not be part of the "experiencing of God." The enlightened model reflects the freedom and openness of Truth that permeates in the various activities of the various disciplines—but emphasizes that Truth is not limited. The enlightened model emphasizes the commitments of the various disciplines, phenomena and the individuals who are in dialogue while simultaneously acknowledging that Truth is everywhere if one permits oneself to be open to it. This model is valuable in that it clarifies the fact that there are not only different kinds of knowing—e.g., physiological, psychological or theological —but finally, that there is one Truth. The enlightened model frees us from the temptation to think that we can contain or control the Truth while inviting us to the on-going, continual acquisition of growth and development.

In summary, this presentation has focused upon how people think in the dialogue of medicine, psychology, and religion. Certainly, other models may be considered. One notes, in the models which have been discussed, that there is a progression toward bridging gaps between the surgeon's table, the analyst's couch and the church's pew. As we progress from the monolithic model to the enlightened model, suspicion and hostility are replaced in affirmation and mutual support. It is suggested that the enlightened model nurtures growth in good health of body, mind and soul, while expanding one's life.

It is noted that the disciplines of medicine, psychology and religion offer much to modern times through their particular insights and perspectives. We find that in the loneliness and helplessness that are part of the encounter with death, the appreciation of these disciplines draws us nearer to one another and, in this way, we are empowered by the fullness of Truth.

Both science and religious professionals have observed what our "divided selves" have yielded—what one priest calls "the fears of nothingness, the horror of emptiness"—or lack of faith—and what a motivational psychologists refers to as "existential sickness"—or having no meaning. In the final analysis, our times demand that helping professionals be open and use the widest possible range of means that are available, working together toward assisting humankind to be not fragmented but whole.

Chapter Two

DEATH AND DYING:
A MEDICAL PERSPECTIVE

Mel Krant

The task that was assigned to me was to talk about the physician and his relationship to people who are dying and the relationship of the physician to the self as well as to the staff.

I think the first message to get across is that we understand the nature of human beings and their present residence on this earth. People can die quite suddenly, and there's been an enormous investment in health care resources to prevent that from happening. This can be witnessed by people losing weight and jogging around reservoirs, throwing away whiskey bottles and stamping out their cigarettes and through various other things which supposedly ought to secure for us a long adventure. And if that doesn't meet anybody's particular situation or if things go wrong with that, almost every hospital in the Commonwealth, if not in the United States, has intensive care units of one sort or the other to bear witness to the enormous technological possibilities of preventing people from dying.

It's not that people do not die in these units, but the intent there is quite clear. The intent of these intensive care units is basically to prevent the death from occurring; and if it does occur, it's because, in fact, technology is short.

The longside view of that is that it will not be long before these misadventures, namely the inability to rescue somebody, will cease, and that whether it be a cardiac death or an expiratory death or any one of these other catastrophic events, certainly an accidental death, poisonous death or what have you, there are certaintudes in the not too distant horizon, through technological advantages, that these

17

particular deaths will cease to be. As that occurs, we'll find that in the twentieth century, the second major alteration in the design of nature has sort of imposed upon the turn of the century to change.

Back about nineteen hundred, as you're aware, death stalked the streets of the United States and the world. But it was mostly children who died from all the infectious disabilities which came with the particular time in which they lived. Children's deaths, though they do occur, are rather rare now, and I'd like to say that one of the extraordinary commodities of the twentieth century has been the alteration of the time when most "deathing" was happening in the United States.

Children seldom die now from the complications and from the issues of which they did die at the turn of the century. The second major change, if we get there before the next century, will be in these acute catastrophic deaths as depicted primarily by accidents and by cardiac illness. These will leave then an extraordinary number of citizens who will grow older and, growing older, will be witness to chronic disabilities, and, as such, then we'll find that the nature of dying will not be acute and sudden, but it will be long and drawn out.

The prototypical adventure along these lines rests in the cancer crisis. Although there is at present extraordinary activity in research and technological activities which are changing the nature of the cancer experience, especially for young people in the United States, the fact seems to be that incidence of cancer is going up; and it will probably continue to be a disease of older citizens—and by older I mean those who are mostly over the age of fifty-five and sixty. The nature of that experience will be that people will slowly die. They'll also be dying, of course, of many other things.

The particular experience I know something about, which I can share, relates to my own thoughts about what that process represents. In the unwanted experience, in the cancer experience, there are two major divisions of the way people counteract and deal with their illness. On the one side are all the efforts which are there for rescue. They begin basically with attempts to uncover the cancer experience rather early in its militancy upon the body: breast self-examination, etc., the searching in the blood, if you will, for various markers, enzymes of various sorts. All of these will indicate to those who examine such tissues and such body fluids that there is an alteration, that there's something wrong somewhere in which, then, the health care system can act. Such things are becoming more and more commonplace and I assume that as time goes along, we all will find ourselves seeking out such information and advice in a systematic manner.

We're covering the possibility of very early disease. The sense then of *DIS*-ease, that which brings a person to see a doctor when he's not feeling well, has already changed and will change further to recognize that the power of scientific medicine will be able to uncover an issue in the body long before a person feels sick. And, therefore, the sense of it will be that you will seek out medical care not because you are ill but because of the potential of something being uncovered before the illness actually starts. Such efforts are already in evidence and will continue to grow in depth as time goes along.

And as that happens, then we will face, as I said before, two things: what can be done when the disease gets apparent, in the line of surgery, in therapy, hemotherapy, chemotherapy and various other drug modalities; and what to do after primary experience. In the nature of what happens in the cancer experience today, it's safe to say that the first assault that takes place upon the individual is probably surgical where it really can be done. And a certain number of limited conditions follow. It's a combination of different modalities including chemotherapy as upfront, priority management.

Now a fair number of people do well for an infinite or indefinite period of time. Not long after that primary experience, through, using "long" in the sense of even months to years, there's a recurrence, and in that recurrence the individual must face again decisions as to what to do at that time, and those decicions become harder as time goes along. Thus, each decicion leads to a second decision and a third decision being done. Now if you have to prolong or rescue individuals in the state that they are in, sooner or later to most individuals who are undergoing this rather extended experience, there comes a moment when they can, if they wish, face a decision as to whether to continue engaging in procedures which will rescue them for some period of time at the expense of being patient and assisted, at the expense of their commitment to giving their bodies over to that process or they seek not to take on that experience any longer.

They seek, in fact, to make some arrangement within whatever compartments there lies in their soul to allow death that sanction, and they will live out a rather different sort of life towards the end of that one. Physicians in most of our major institutions, it's been my experience, do not have a terribly comfortable time permitting that latter experience to occur. And it seems to occupy or it seems to sift through a number of different relevancies as to what that experience represents.

First of all, in fact, to understand it fully, I think it is wise to realize that there is nothing romantic in the experience of dying of cancer. Cancer is not only a disease for the medically disorganized tissues. Cancer is a disorder which presents to the individuals an experience of great suffering. If you ask most individuals who have been through a cancer experience, either inside of themselves at some point or in their families, what the image of that experience is, I think you come out with a fairly universal set of orders, with a set of visions as to what that experience means.

There's scarcely a family that has not, at some level or another, gone through a cancer experience with some member in that family. What other experiences, what visions do you have when the word "cancer" appears?

Woman: Fear.

Dr. Krant: Fear?

Woman: Fear.

Dr. Krant: Cancer as a sentence. Death itself is inherent, in the works. Is that what you're saying?

Woman: Yeah.

Dr. Krant: Debilitation. Different from death but still fear.

Man: I was going to say the pain and suffering. Someone suffering in a long, drawn out preiod.

Dr. Krant: Do you equate those two characteristics, pain and suffering, as the same thing?

Man: No. Pain is something that is sharp and intense, and the suffering is something that gradually declines.

Dr. Krant: Can you define, think further about your own sense of what suffering means?

Man: A long process of debilitation, I'd add. That's the best I can figure.

Dr. Krant: Okay. Please.

Woman: I think more of a mental anguish. The suffering comes more with the mental suffering, I think.

Dr. Krant: Would you care to paint tht picture a bit more vividly; what is the mental anguish?

Woman: The thought of leaving your family.

Dr. Krant: The thought of leaving your family. Okay. Any other comments?

Man: You said the helplessness of a part of you.

Dr. Krant: Helplessness to do what?

Man: Helplessness for the one who's suffering or has the cancer.

Dr.Krant: What is it about the suffering that they can't help?

Man: Well, just that you don't feel that there's anything you can do to cure it. And that you're inevitably missing this person.

2nd Man: You could say possible incapacitation of the patient and self and the mental anguish of the family that involves—

Dr. Krant: The incapacity to think. The possibility that person is changed; the person can't do. At some line or some level those functions are necessary for reasonable living, a reasonable life.

2nd Man: Yes. The person, let's say, who's been very active all his life, doing for himself, all of a sudden realizes that he has to rely upon other people, and this creates some kind of a problem in itself; of just lying in bed being fully aware of what's going on and the inability, again, to take care of himself.

Woman: Denial.

Dr. Krant: Denial of—

Woman: Denial that it's really happening to me; or that I'll wake up tomorrow and it won't be there.

Dr. Krant: Well, we can go on and on. I think that if you look at individual thoughts that people have about the cancer experience, it is seldom that one brings out anything good about it. It is fraught with an imaging system which is all negative. In fact, if you think about the word—the word "cancer," does anyone know from where the word first appears in the English language? It's in the sixteenth century, according to the Oxford Dictionary, when the word first began to be used in English. But tell me what other overtones that word implies besides its biology. Can you think of other terms or other ways in our general life that the word is applied?

Woman: In the heart of pain, the crab; and you think of it as a disease.

Dr. Krant: What sort of animal is a crab? Pleasant, fun sort of thing to have around? Would you go out and get your child a pet crab? What kind of animal is a crab? Scavenger! Scary. Sort of secretive, crawling. Bottom of the ocean. Not very visible. More nightly than daily. Coming out at different times. Certainly not a pleasant thought—usually these are the thoughts associated with it. In fact, we even have a disease called "the crab" which we associate with a different form of malevolence. But, nevertheless, the idea of the crab is certainly correct. Any other thoughts about cancer? Have you ever heard it expressed politically? What was Vietnam on that attitude? Have you ever heard it expressed: the cancer or malignancy?

The word has endless overtones and they're all evil, dirty, filthy, rotten, slimy, sneaky. Those sorts of things which come at you when you're least expecting it. They invade from behind. They're by far the backside of this human experience. And here's a word, then, that's so fraught with indigence and when we apply it to disease process in people you can imagine the associative symbolic things that go with this word. Very few people look on the cancer experience as being something enlightening, embolding, growing, associative, clearing, satisfactory. And yet it can be all those things. However, without getting too much into my romantic sense of this, it's safe to say that the cancer disease experience, as people go through it, is a rotten, painful, difficult thing for some. Not for all.

It seems to me that most people have two or three extraordinary fears about the cancer experience. Part of that fear is the fear that we will be changed as human beings.

No longer being the independent, self-sufficient, self-powerful people whom others can rely upon. In fact, I think you heard several people talk about incapacity. With cancer no longer can we be that human being who is valued or whom we can value ourselves. We now have to rely on others for their support rather than see ourselves as being a primary investor in the world. Images which we're not comfortable with, especially in the ways we've grown up and rationalized with what our society preaches as high values.

The cancer experience is seen as one of extraordinary pain. There are very few people who, when asked what is their greatest fear of cancer, do not respond that they fear it will produce a pain that is not livable. And I think terms like 'helplessness,' which I hear people saying, are oftentimes associated with an image of people watching a loved one writhing, furiously, in savage pain and having nothing that can contain it. Nothing that can stop that pain. And the second usual image that one has of the cancer experience is one of loss of body. A skinning process. A thinning, weeding out. So that the wonderfulness of flesh, the thing which allows us to walk and to sprightly get about our business is destroyed. The being then gives way to this erosion of flesh, people losing weight, getting thinner and thinner and thinner, and they get blacker and weaker and weaker.

And it's those two extrordinary margins which are surrounded by symbols of what the cancer experience means to many; and it carries, innately, the word of death. That cancer and death are co-existing terms, I think is also apparently clear, and it was in the original use of the word that it was seen that way; that the cancerous or the cankerous sense was not only an evil growth but it was a growth of death. Death was a malignant plague which went along with the cancer experience, and therefore, whatever death is and death means, the process of dying, the vividness of knowing that you must go through that experience calls upon your individual end-lessness, wrapped into the realization that the body may well have extraordinary matters of diminishment and of pain and of other kinds of commodities, other kinds of evils which we no longer, and with which we never have felt comfortable.

For example, things such as not being able to catch one's breath because lungs are being invaded, fluid is accumulating in various pockets. Being breathless is a terrifying state of the human exper-ience. Not knowing where and when your next breath's going to come from and how it can be facilitated are things which terrify. The whole idea of perhaps choking—choking because you can't clear secretions.

And now, it's another very terrifying image which we have: in-vasion, not only of the body but of the brain, giving rise to a state of confusion, disorganization; giving way to, in fact, being unaware. Convulsive disorders produce their own mayhem as well. The reali-zation that no part of this human experience of ours is invulnerable from attack in the cancer experience can lead to misery.

The nature, then, of going through that experience is such that there are individuals—there are many individuals, in fact, who, given any opportunity to be rescued by whatever form or existing or ex-perimental therapeutics that may exist, seek out and must have that opportunity. So, it is not surprising that we find a deep investment in many of our health care institutions in experimental designs, in-novative, new ways of attacking the late stage cancer process, so that people can feel that they can fight back on some levels, or at least feel that there's an investment by federal agencies, by government monies, by health care resource systems, as such, which will not sit back and let this happen without some attack on the process, without some hope that somewhere relief will be found through the existing knowledge that man has and further knowledge as it grows.

If you are watching anything these days about genetic engineer-ing and the onca gene and all that's going on in that sense, you'll notice that no matter what else is talked about—the onca gene or the DNA recombinant structures which are being made and the change in genetic disorganization, the sense that "this may be a treat-ment for cancer," is stated on every single case. That disease still rules in the sense that the feeling we must have, as a society, that we are being protected or, at least, that attack is being made to prevent this process from being everlasting with us is very dominant in our news media, and certainly is paying the salaries of large numbers of people in investigative laboratories throughout the country. There are investigative programs that the federal government maintains in Washington with constant invitation to people with various kinds of cancer who will be looked after, their transportation paid for, their hotel maintained by the government for the sake of investigation. All this continues on.

At the same level there's been a growing witness or a growing feeling of what was not being done, that there had to be some humanist experience proclaimed that would alter the way people died in the United States, especially from cancer. Those of you who have followed at all what has gone on with the hospice program for the last ten or fifteen years know that it finally reached a climax in the federal legislation; the enactment bill that was made through social security monies this past year will allow appropriate organizations invested with the proper credentials to get so-called hospice care.

The hospice notion takes as its primary effort that doing battle against cancer is not enough. That one must also do battle against inhumanness, and oddly enough, it defines "inhumanness" as too much care; it defines "inhumanness" as too much experimentation; "humanness" as somehow the gathering together of appropriate forces to allow a person to slip out of life and out of suffering in a warm, respected, home, organized way.

And so we find that simultaneous to the attack motif, the idea that aggressive militancy against cancer and all that it stands for have got to occur on one level of government expenditure; we have this other theme which has arisen and which has grown that we must pay more attention to: humanistically letting people go. When you speak, however, about humanistically letting people die, it gets to be a bit confusing, because what tends to appear is a romantic notion that all you need to do is gather a rather substantial group of caring individuals together and that each and every citizen can then slip out of a life in a warm, passionate, compassionate setting with the ease of everybody else. Let me tell you that is sheer garbage! Because, in fact, the cancer experience and dying is and can be brutal.

All the things that people fear are reasonable. They are bad. You see people dying who cannot catch their breath, and they stay that way, suffering in anguish for long periods of time before they finally die. And they do this probably as badly at home with lots of people around them as they do in hospitals, giving rise to those of us who make house calls and have to be in attendance to such people, of living on telephones endlessly because of the fear that families have overstated what's going on with one of their loved ones at home. It gives rise to endless attacks of infection and having to make a decision of whether to rehospitalize somebody, start an antibiotic, get some culture or what the hell to do at that moment. What is the decision to be on a day to day basis?

It calls for endless vigilence, a realization that the pathway is not smooth and that people—when people are even in the most humane of places, at home—it is a difficult and oftentimes painful experience. Is it a better experience than being in the hospital? Perhaps. For some it could be, but not for all. Can the experience be alleviated and ameliorated so that it becomes more peaceful? The answer to that, if I may say, is yes, but it requires an extraordinary amount of attention and money and services to get in what is necessary to ease that process at home and the realization that it works best if there are hospital back-up beds available to put people for shorter or longer periods of time into an institution to be covered for various kinds of contingencies which can take place.

There is nothing romantic about dying with cancer. It is a difficult process and requires an extraordinary pathway of resources to have this happen comfortably at home. It is recognized, too, that when talking about incapacity, oftentimes our present families, flung widely as they are with daughters in one place and sons in another and very few folks around in the form of siblings, suddenly are called upon to return back home to bear witness and to participate in the day and night needs that these families have if they are going to care for the loved one back home, disrupting their lives and their commitments to their particular kinds of growth and development of their careers.

It's not that families will not do that but they can't do it for very long. And we find that in the modern America scene a daughter in California will want to know, "Do I come back home? Or do I wait 'til next week? And if I wait 'til next week, will it be too late? Will mother have died? But if I come home now and she doesn't die, what do I then do, because I have my family back in Califoria and I have to go back there?" This kind of insecurity, of doubtfulness, of uncertainty is a reflection, basically, not only of the social structuring which we've done in the United States and the scattering of families, but the realization that we are really ill-equipped to make very clear witness to what the slow dying of cancer really can be like.

We have to formulate, I think, not only a biological program but a disease-oriented program to look at what we're going to do in the process of caring for the citizens, those in the present and those in the future, who will probably have to undergo these things. But I think it calls for a larger kind of understanding in ourselves of what we really think about and what we really want to have happen should the experience happen to us. What kind of lifestyle, what kind of interrelationship with health care systems is most advantageous? What do we really want from others as we go through this experience,and more than that, what is it that we really want for ourselves?

Now you wouldn't be suprised in that kind of firmament to realize that there must be growing in the United States a rather large movement toward self-termination; that is, the notion that if one has to go through such experiences, one ought to have some help either from the government, again, or from health care people out there to help us terminate our lives when we want to terminate them so that, in fact, we do not have to go through all the biological, psychological and familial torment which we see and understand is so much a part of the experience of the late stage cancer dying.

Those of you who watch television may remember that it wasn't terribly long ago that one of the major networks was invited into somebody's home to see a fifty-eight-year-old woman with breast cancer take her life in a very organized party which, in fact, the network thought was ridiculous and grotesque but participated. We watched this whole experience take place right in front of our eyes— a kind of Roman Carnival out of the catacomb days taking place in a very modern American ethos. Anyway, that experience, I think, caused the realization that that motif is growing in the United States. Call it humanistic. Call it barbaric.

I certainly don't wish to argue one way or the other, except to make you aware that such organizations, in California primarily, but granted, all over, and certainly here in New England, going under various names—there is one called the hemlock approach named after you know who—will send out literature and will tell people what drugs to use and where they can get these drugs in order to self-terminate when they wish to do it independent of the medical system.

Let me just sum up by saying that most of us will grow older since young and middle-aged death is getting less. Most of us will not die from acute disorders as time goes along; that technology will be with us and, I suspect, will be ever more prominent in altering that experience for us. Most of us will experience disease which will slowly result in deaths. In many ways which I didn't touch upon, they have available today commodius apparatus to care for pain so that we can virtually, not absolutely, but, virtually promise that with appropriate application patients will suffer much less pain in the experience of dying.

Question: And how does the hospice help people die in a more conducive way? How does it help them cope with their pain and suffering?

Dr. Krant: Now we have those movements that take the incentive in the United States—buildings have come up with beds in them so that people can speed their dying times in such settings. There are no such buildings in Boston. There are a fair number of opinions that we could set aside a small number of beds to be part of a hospice experience, especially for cancer patients.

There's a very large one at the University of Massachusetts. I don't think that there are any such in the Boston area—in the immediate Boston area. Their experience has been old people stay at home by bringing together both nursing, medical, psychological and volunteer resources to help both patients and families cope. Cope medically, how decisions are made by physicians and others coming into homes and by rather significant corps of volunteers who will help families and their members deal with various experiences about their dying. The Brookline hospice is just one of these—one of many hospices in this area which are concentrating primarily on helping people at home by bringing in the resources which I mentioned before.

Question: Doctor, do you see any danger in the fact that these hemlock societies mean that people are going to terminate their lives before any real efforts are made to save them?

Dr. Krant: I would rather not answer that. I think mainly because part of the issue is whether physicians will make available materials they don't think occur. Oddly enough, you would think that if one wanted to kill one's self there would be endless easier ways of doing it without asking anybody's help. There are enough tall buildings around. There are enough ropes around and a slew of guns, what have you, to take care of people's needs in that regard. But most sick people don't have the energy to resort to that. They seek out medication for those things, and the gatekeepers of those medications are physicians. Therefore, the question becomes toward the medical people, are they going to participate? Should that patient say, "Hey, I would like—" Or, "Can you help me get—" what have you . . . I'd like to be the determinator of when that should occur. I don't even begin to question the religious relationship of such actions, especially in the synagogue—how physicians behave when asked to comply with such requests of individuals who ask that they be terminated one way or the other or self-terminated by themselves before actual death occurs. The physicians' response to that—you'd find it very hard to get physicians to discuss it openly. For the very simple reason that in the Commonwealth of Massachusetts anybody that facilitates the death of another, even by a minute, is under engagement by the law. It's a criminal law. And one could easily find a good attorney who could issue it in terms of manslaughter, but I don't think you'd find anybody that would say, "Hey, I do this all the time, but we weren't sure about what people would think about that." That's another risk.

Dr. Chirban: Dr. Krant, am I correct in understanding that you're saying that the medical profession understands that life will end generally in a slow chronic process? Have they accepted that ? I get the impression when you speak that that's an accepted understanding in the medical profession. And are there more creative approaches to extending life? For example, in the popular trade press there's a book called, *Life Extension*, But are there serious thoughts, more creative thoughts, around possibilities of dealing with keeping human beings alive longer?

Dr. Krant: Let me argue that by having two theoretical arguments about how life should be as time goes along. *The New England Journal of Medicine* carried a treatise about three years ago on the so-called court wrangling of the sphere of life. It says, basically, that disease will be wiped out. That people would live to the maximum their bodies can live, perhaps a hundred and five, a hundred and ten years. And like the one horse shades of Walker Bates' poem, we simply all just grow older gracefully and the day would come when we go to sleep and don't wake up. And that comes from a group of theoretical experiments that started by Hetrich and others about the capabilities of individual selves to sustain life in organized bodies that come together and the realization of the expectation that we have less disease as time goes along. We would wipe out disease, yet more bodies would simply go on and on and on. And suddenly, push, they'd end up in a cloud of dust.

More lately there have been, I think, much more realistic assessments which point to the fact that acute disease and sudden death is getting less and less in the United States. And that chronic disease is growing in numbers, and that as people get older, what's going to happen is that chronic disease isn't going to disappear; it's that there'll be more and more of it. And more and more of it basically means that health care resources and expenditures are going to grow in the care of such phenomenon in the same way as we've moved away from worrying whether children are going to die from measles, etc., which they no longer do. When I was a child, my mother loves to still tell me, they say that it was only by the skin of somebody's teeth that I didn't die of scarlet fever.

In the same way, I think, a few coronary diseases will probably disappear. Acute, traumatic deaths will not. Car accidents and things like that will go on, but as acute, sudden deaths from heart disease, etc., disappear, more and more people get beyond that, what they will face are the chronic disorders and key among them—I think the evidence is overwhelming—key among them will be cancer. That all solutions for the cancer problem will be for young cancer and not for the kind of disorder which we'll feel later in life, as well as other kinds of disabling disease. Alzheimer's disease, senility, a whole rash of rather severe, chronic problems that old people can get. As time goes along we will simply see more and more and more. Do doctors agree that there will be more and more chronic disease with time? Most of them do. That is, most theoretical biologists who wonder about what makes the human live will tend to see that.

Dr.Chirban: I was asking that question related to a futuristic understanding of health care. In other words, might the extension of life be perceived in other, more creative ways?

Dr. Krant: Well, I can't answer that. Let me tell you that at Deaconness, they've just done their third liver transplant. As that kind of alteration of the body proceeds, you can transplant kidneys, livers, eyes, hearts, maybe even brains. It becomes commonplace, and I think it will become more and more commonplace as time goes along. Once you initiate such biological adventures, it's very hard to turn around and to stop them; especially when technology is available. On a very theoretical note, I can tell you that one of the things that frightens a number of people like that is the whole area of genetic engineering, the nature of what new illnesses are going to be introduced by meddling with this particular picture. That's a whole unknown. Nobody knows that.

Chapter Three

DEATH AND DYING: CLINICAL-PSYCHOLOGICAL PERSPECTIVE

Gerald Koocher

I would like to complement some of the things that Dr. Krant mentioned by talking a little bit about "the adaptational process." As a psychologist, I've long been interested in human coping and adaptation, and probably I've spent much of my time dealing with the survivors, that is, not only children who survive a life-threatening experience but family members who go on living after a death has occurred. I'd like to spend some time now talking about that type of adaptation.

I would like to tell you what one parent told me, because it probably is the only answer I've ever heard to question Dr. Krant's question about is there anything good about cancer? A mother told me once there was something good about cancer, and that is it gave you a chance to say good-bye. This was a mother who was attending a group—an organization known as the Compassionate Friends. This is an organization, a self-help group, of families that have lost a child.

There was this mother who sent her eight-year-old son off to school one morning and he got hit by a car. He was killed, and she never saw him again. One of the things that bothered her as she sat and listened to other parents in the group talk about their losses, including parents who had lost a child in chronic illness was the time factor. She said, "You had a chance to talk about it. You had a chance to communicate some important things that I wish I could have said but really didn't have the opportunity to express."

This brings me to a point about the importance of communicating among family members when someone is at risk for dying or

31

when someone is near death—if not just in general. People often ask me, "How have you gotten interested in working with dying patients and studying death? Isn't that a rather morbid topic?"

I have probably spent the last ten or eleven years talking with kids a lot about dying and what makes things die—and talking with terminally ill children, adolescents and young adults. I got into it quite by accident. I was in graduate school. I was looking for a dissertation topic and I happened to be assigned to work with a six-year-old girl named Helen who had been brought to the clinic by her parents because she was now refusing to go to bed at night for some reason. So we did an evaluation. We couldn't particularly find anything wrong in the sense of psychopathology in Helen's family, but we decided to do some exploratory play therapy and one day Helen picked up the toy telephone and told me about Mr. So and so, the next door neighbor, who had had a heart attack, fell out of bed and died. She wasn't sure about dying, but she knew that it was something that was not good. She knew nothing about heart attacks, but if falling out of bed could make it happen, nobody was going to get her into her bed.

That got me interested in the magical types of ideas that children have about dying and what makes things die. It occurred to me that if we understood a little more about that, we might be able to do some things to help especially children cope better with losses. I ended up interviewing lots of kids at different ages to find out what they thought about death.

When I first began the study, people said, "Are you going to talk about that? You're going to terrify them!" That was especially told to me by one school principal who didn't want me to interview the children in his school. I later discovered that his son had been critically ill. Interestingly enough, a lot of the fears, anxieties and inhibitions that we hear about are more a function of adult fears than children's fears; and, in fact, when one sits down and talks with children about concerns in a supportive climate, and in a matter-of-fact way, one gets very interesting answers.

I will just tell you a little bit about different age levels and death. And I'm going to splice it into three age levels because there's some important intellectual changes that affect what children understand.

According to a lot of theory one important stage is when the child is under six years old. What happens at around six- or seven-years-old is that kids begin for the first time to be able to put themselves in another person's shoes and understand another person's experiences.

This was well illustrated to me when I was asking kids, "How long do you think you'll live? How old do you think you'll be when you die?" One six-year-old told me she was going to live to be seven. Another six-year-old said to me, "Well, how old are you?" At the time I was twenty-one and I told him that. "Well, I'm going to live to be twenty-two."

Youngsters in this age group, under six, also are prone to magical thinking. If you ask them what makes things die, they'll tell you one may get poisoned or hit by a car or fall out of an airplane. But you could also get killed: "if you go swimming alone," "if you take medicine that your mom doesn't give you," "if you eat dirt." One youngster told me you can die from "styrofoam cups." I said, "How?" "If you chew on them too much." One little girl told me, "Raw hot dogs could kill you." She said, "Mom told me that." Well, that's exactly what happens. It's the internalized parent speaking and magical thinking.

Sometimes there are interesting misunderstandings. I had a youngster who was seven-years-old who went into a funeral Mass following the stillborn sibling's death. I asked him if children ever die. He said, "Yes, children can die if God wants them up in heaven." A very interesting answer. It had not yet occurred to him—I wonder what would happen to him if someone said to him. "God loves you." Oh-oh! Will He want me up in heaven, too?

One of the recommendations that I always give to people who are going to try to explain death to children, let's say under five or six, is that after you tell them what you think you have told them, ask them to repeat it back again: "And pretend I'm one of your friends and I want to know. What will you tell me?" This same youngster, who gave you that information when I said, "How old do people live to be?"—told me, "You could live to be a hundred million-years-old, like a cave man." Well, they were studying dinosaurs and cave men that lived a hundred million years ago. Again, the inability to use that kind of information can be pretty interesting.

Another thing that happens that is significant is that it is not until around age six that children are really sure that death is irreversible. Again,this is because they can't understand things that they haven't experienced themselves. This is a result of the fact that they can't take on the role of other people yet; they're not sure about death because they've never experienced it. That's why we never tell a youngster that dying is like falling asleep, because that is something they've experienced and that could be terrifying. It's important to explain things like when you die, you don't breathe and you don't eat and you don't drink and so forth. Because, they reason, "If I'm breathing, I'm not dead."

Something else that would happen is you might ask a five-year-old, "Can you make something that's dead come back to life?" and the youngster would say, "Well, yeah. Call the doctor. Take him to the emergency room." I had one say, "Give him chicken soup." Now can you imagine if a youngster believes that, what's going to happen when someone dies?

It's important that they get an explanation because one of the things that will happen is they will keep asking and asking. I worked with a five-year-old who died of cancer and the mother requested help to explain to the three-year-old what had happened. And I helped the mother to formulate a specific kind of explanation that would not be threatening. "Jennifer had cancer. You don't have cancer, Amanda. The doctors couldn't make Jennifer's cancer better and that's why she died." And I cautioned the mother that the little one would be asking the same question over and over. That wasn't disbelief; that was an attempt to master the situation—to gain control of it. The mother reported that the three-year-old would keep asking, and she'd listen and about the second or third sentence, she'd walk away. She'd heard enough. She was checking to see if the story had changed. One of the first questions that children have when someone dies is, "Will that happen to me?" The second thing that will occur, especially if it's an adult or someone who's taking care of them is, "Did I do it?"

There is the youngster who's mad at the teacher and the teacher has a heart attack; the youngster wonders magically, "Was it something I did?" Or a child has a fight with his brother and says, "I wish you were dead." Then, the brother goes out and gets hit by a car. He wonders, "Did I do it?" It's important to try to address those issues with children directly.

Sometimes the youngster won't always say what's on his or her mind. When talking to a child who's lost a sibling, I'll say to them, "You know, I talk to lots of kids who worry about people dying, and one thing that they think about is, 'Is that going to happen to me?' If it's a cancer death, it's possible to reassure them: "Well, you don't have it. We had the doctor examine you and you don't have cancer so you don't have to worry about that now."

But for this three-year-old, asking the question, "Mommy,

Daddy, is anything going to happen to you." And Mommy and Daddy said, "Well, we're all going to die some day, but we're both well and we hope we're not going to die for a long, long time. But if anything should happen to us, there will still be people to take care of you. There'll be Auntie Robin and Uncle Bob and Grandma and Grandpa." And so we helped script this so a child would know that there was some nurturance there. The mother, Fran, became frightened after overhearing her daughter's reaction. Later, she heard the three-year-old playing with her dolls about "How Mommy Died." The little girl told the doll that Mommy died and so they were going to have to go stay with Grandma or Auntie Robin. The mother telephoned me. My advice: "Don't worry. She's trying to reassure herself that she still has people to take care of her." The game disappeared after a few days. The mastery exercises that very young children go through are not at all different from that.

Now as people get older, we begin to say that we don't think like that; and usually most of us don't. But at times, we still do, especially when we're under stress. Kubler-Ross talks about stages which people go through in mourning and grief stages; for example, the feelings of insecurity, anger, bargaining: "If only I go to the hospital today, I'll live a little bit longer." No degree of professionalism or intellectualism can protect you from those feelings of guilt and loss and sadness.

I recall the very first patient I ever worked with, who died after 1972, was a six-year-old boy who had eplastic anemia which is a disease that was not treatable. I began working with him in February, and he died the following April. The week he died, he was in the hospital in sterile isolation because of his susceptibility to infection, and I was home in bed with mononucleosis.

I don't remember the dream I had the night after I heard he had died, but it must still be threatening for me because I can never recall exactly what happened in the dream. But I remember the sense of it very well: if you had been at work this week, he would have lived another week. Magical thinking! And I knew it was magical. I knew that it didn't make sense. And I woke up and said, "Now I know I'm a psychologist; I know why I was thinking that. I wished this would happen and my wish didn't come true." But, still, it happens, and one cannot escape from that, and one should not try to deny one's humanness and recognize that you can't be out of touch with that.

People say to me sometimes, "Well, how do you manage to work with dying patients all the time and not go crazy?" One of the ways that you do that is you don't spend all of your time working with dying patients. You do other things. Whatever you do, it's important to experience yourself as a person in a variety of spheres, whether it's as a parent or a teacher or a researcher or through some other avenues. So, when the unavoidable, sad events happen, you can deal with them as sad events, and it does not have a pervasive, overwhelming impact on your life.

There is one element of working with seriously ill children and with people who suffer losses which really has enriched my own life as a person and as a psychotherapist. It gives me a good sense of values and what's important in people's lives. I often see in my practice what I would call neurotic patients—people who have conflicts or struggles that they keep getting into over and over and over again. And they come to you for help, but they really don't want to break out of that way of responding.

When you are with a family when someone in the family is dying, the motivation is there, the time limit is sensed, and people are able to accomplish a considerable amount of relating to each other and dealing with issues over a relatively short period of time. The potential from being there as a clergyman, as a physician, as a psychologist, as a caring other, to help people during that time is an extremely enriching experience—to have people let you share this intimate point in their life and to help them cope with that period.

There is one thing that happened to me about five years ago which I try to think of when I'm feeling particularly frustrated or annoyed with the facts in life, to help put events in perspective. That was one day I had about four or five years ago when I was asked to come in and talk with the parents of a ten-year-old boy who had a Burkitt's lymphoma which was not responding to treatment. Burkitt's lymphoma is a particularly virulent type of tumor which, when it is not under control, doubles in bulk every twenty-four hours. And this youngster had been hospitalized for several months and had several major surgeries to try to deal with the cancer, chemotherapy and so forth. And it was now clear to the physician treating him that they had nothing more to offer to fight the disease. They could control the pain, but the disease was going to prove terminal. They shared this information with the parents, and the parents wanted somehow to communicate this to their son, but they did not know quite how to do that. It's not easy, as you might imagine.

I sat with them for two hours as we talked about presenting this to him and talked about whether he wanted to try experimental drugs and things of that sort. And I had another rather powerful hour and a half session sitting together with the two parents and the eleven-year-old as we talked about all of these things.

I then left my office at the cancer institute and went out to the suburbs to an office where I was working in private practice with a group of other psychologists and psychiatrists. I was to see a new patient that afternoon, and the patient was brought in by her mother. I should say that the first family was the family of a truck driver and housewife from a very poor town in the rural part of the state. And now I was going to see the daughter of a Vassar graduate mother, MIT graduate father, a very well-to-do family. They were bringing their daughter, same age, in to see the psychologist because, as the mother put it, "She won't wear dresses to school! She insists on wearing her dirty jeans." Typical mother. I wanted to say, "Hey, lady, you're crazy to struggle with your child over something that trivial." But I often call up that memory when my car is overheating on the expressway or some other life event is happening, to remind myself about some of the things that are important.

I would like to share with you about helping families cope and, particularly, helping the family members who will go on, who will be survivors after the death, to adapt. I shall present the scenarios of two families that coped in very different ways. And highlight some of the issues which are important.

One family which we can call the Smith family had a six-year-old child who was diagnosed as having a brain tumor shortly after Christmas one year. A few weeks later, the doctors completed their diagnosis and were able to inform the family that the tumor was at a location in the brain that made it inoperable. They could offer some radiation treatment to slow its progress, but after a year or so the child was probably going to succumb to the tumor. Within a week after getting that news, Dad walked up to the doctor in charge of the case and offered to sign an autopsy consent form—offering to give the doctor permission to perform an autopsy. Physicians like to be able to study the body to determine the progress of the tumor and so forth. This happened only a few days after the diagnosis when the doctors told him that the child was not going to die for several months. The father also began to talk about the child—in the child's presence—in the third person. It was no longer "Joey." It was "him." The mother was furious. She approached the social worker psychologist for support. The father listened to these complaints and then said, "Well, you are over-emotional. You're over-reacting.

You've got to get perspective on this. When my mother died, you cried more about it than I did.''

What we are seeing were two dramatically different coping styles—that did not fit well together, and in fact, were causing some friction in their relationship. Shift gears for a minute and let's talk about another family which we'll call the Harris family. The Harris' daughter developed a meningitis infection, a severe brain infection. She was rushed into the hospital and was placed in the intensive care unit. One of the parents was always by the bedside but they didn't seem to communicate with each other. It was as though there was an unspoken agreement that when one would arrive the other would leave. The mother in this case also complained that she was feeling unsupported by her husband. He didn't seem to want to deal with the seriousness of their daughter's illness. Again, we tried to organize a family meeting.

When the wife said that to her husband in a meeting she noted that he had been taking long walks in the woods near the family's home and crying to himself because he did not want to burden other family members with the sadness about the daughter's illness and possible death. It was a protective mechanism. He was going to try and shelter the other people in the family from his grief but, at the same time, was not responsive to their grief.

Both of these children died, but different things happened in the families. In the Smith family, where the youngster had the brain tumor, the parents were separated within a few days after the death and were divorced after a few months. In the other family, the couple is still married and has a strong sense of support from each other. Once the communication door was opened for the Harrises, the father did not feel the need to protect the family members any more, and in fact they were able to share their feelings and be supportive.

I can't say to you whether Mr. and Mrs. Smith were coping better than the Harrises. Maybe each of them was coping fine in his or her own way, but they were coping dys-synchronously. There was no harmony in the coping styles. One of the things that this has taught us about is the importance early in a relationship to open the lines of communication and to make it possible for people to talk to each other.

There's an interesting development cycle, a kind of reversal that occurs. We often hear parents saying, "I don't want to talk to my child about death," because that's frightening and it's stressful and so forth. I think the stresses are often in the mind of the adult. It reverses about sixty or seventy years later when the elder parent is the one who's sick and the children come in and say, "We don't want our elder parent who's just been diagnosed as having a terminal illness to know about it. We want to protect him." Human beings are remarkably resilient creatures and they're very capable of protecting themselves. If you tell someone something he doesn't want to hear, he won't hear it. People do not fall apart or disintegrate when you tell them difficult things. They may choose to ignore you, they may choose to deal with it, but they don't fall apart. By not raising the issue, you sometimes create more of a problem than you do by dealing with it.

In closing, I'd just like to share one other little vignette with you, just to illustrate some of the ways in which you can present material at a level a child is capable of understanding, even under stressful circumstances, and still be helpful. I was working with one little boy who was six-years-old and who was being treated for cancer. It finally became clear after an extended period of treatment that he was going to succumb to his illness. Again, the parents wanted to try and make a presentation to him. Now they wanted to go in and tell him that he was going to die, that they were going to try to support him as much as possible.

Well, something that's very important before you try to communicate that information to a child is that you have to find out about the social, cultural and psychological ecology of the family. I sat with them for two hours and we talked about what their beliefs were about death and dying. Were religious values important to them? Is this something they wanted to speak about? How were they going to present this? This was a Catholic family who had very clear religious beliefs and those beliefs had already been communicated to the child. He had attended church, Sunday school and so forth. We decided to talk to the youngster about his death but agreed that he wasn't going to be left alone. They were going to be with him the whole time. They wanted to reassure him that nothing was going to hurt. And if he hurt, the doctors could give him medicine to help take care of the pain. They also were going to try to answer all his questions.

His concerns were, "I will miss you. I won't have anybody to take care of me." They told him that God would take care of him, and that some day the whole family would be together again. Until the whole family could get together again, God would take care of him. He thought about that for a minute and then he said, "I don't know God." The family told him, "Well, you knew Aunt Helen" (Aunt Helen had died). "And Aunt Helen will take care or you until Mommy and Daddy arrive." He seemed to accept that. The parents left. Later that afternoon, I came to see him and he was very sad and said to me, "I hate Aunt Helen!" "I don't want to die." One can deal with such statements on many levels. We talked about how sad it was to think about those very scary things that people talk about, but that we were going to take care of him. And, I added, "By the way, there were children in heaven, too, and he didn't have to hang out with Aunt Helen."

But there are many ways of, again, trying to present the climate in a manner that's responsive because if no one opened the door to talk to him, he still would have known he was feeling weaker. He would have known that he was getting weaker. He would have known that he was getting sicker. But he would have felt he was frightening other people. I think one of the difficult things is to overcome that burden. His parents said to me afterwards, "You know, once we talked to him about the really hard thing, that we were going to lose him and how sad we were about that, there was nothing else to talk about. We could really be there and be supportive of him. We didn't have to worry that he was going to ask us the really hard question that we were afraid to answer because the hardest point had already been dealt with."

I think that's an important thing to keep in mind—one which many of the writers on death and dying talk about. It's opening that door to communication. If you have a chance that you know someone is seriously ill, if you know someone who is at risk of dying, that should be a signal to you to seize the opportunity. Unfortunately, the vast majority of deaths that occur in the under fifteen age group occur, as Dr. Krant suggested, through accidents or birth defects where the child is either too young to communicate with or the death occurs in such a way that communication is not possible. So my closing message to you would be to take advantage of the opportunity to communicate, because I'm convinced that it not only helps the dying individual to cope better and to feel better, but it certainly helps the survivors to cope a lot better too.

Question: How do you deal with a child that already knows that he or she's going to die before the doctor says, "You're going to die."? My cousin had cystic fibrosis. One morning, as a seven-year-old, she wakes up and she goes to my grandmother and she says,

"Gram, I'm going to die before I reach nine-years-old." She just said it. She said God told her or she dreamt it or something like that, and she did die before she was nine-years-old. But how do you talk to a child like that? What do you tell him or her?

Dr. Koocher: I teach a course at the medical school called Care of the Patient with Terminal Illness; one of the most frightening questions that any physician can hear is, "Am I going to die?" But it is only frightening when a patient is dying. If you can reassure a patient that they're not dying, that's great. But the interesting part is if a patient asks you, they probably know the answer. And if you can recognize that, it takes some of the stress away. The second thing is that often the physician or the person who hears that comment is afraid to say, "Yes, it's true," because they're afraid that they have nothing to offer. But truth and emotional support are things that are very important that can be offered.

I was calling the hospital one Sunday afternoon for a sixteen-year-old leukemia patient who had relapsed. When you relapse, that means his prognosis dropped from being a fifty-fifty chance of being cured to a less than five percent chance. He was taking medication that was making him vomit and he was saying to the staff, "I'm going to die; I'm going to die." The staff, thinking that he knew his prognosis was worse now, didn't want to deal with it and called me in. I started talking with them. Well, it became very clear that what he was saying in between vomiting was that he was afraid he was going to aspirate—swallow some vomit, choke to death. He knew that the change in prognosis was not good. But he also knew he wasn't dying right then. It's important to know what the question is that's being asked. If the patient is feeling weaker and asks you if they're dying, it might be a test to see how honest and direct and supportive you're going to be with him.

When we deal with kids who have cystic fibrosis, I don't feel it's necessary to tell a five- or six-year-old, especially if they're well, that they're dying. We tell them that cyctic fibrosis is a serious disease. People can die from it. That's why it's important that you take your medication and do your physical therapy and so forth. But in giving them that kind of message, you do open a door. I mean, you tell them, "We know people can die from this disease. So, if you're thinking about that, if you're worrying, I hope you'll say it." Another thing which is evident among people who work with dying patients is that there's dying and there's dying.

You know, once you're born, you start dying. now that's not

just a philosophical point, but Dr. Krant made the point that some people think that cancer is a death sentence. He was sort of charitable. He didn't remind you that one in four of us, twenty-five percent of the people in this room, are going to get cancer sometime in his or her life. Only one in three of those is going to die from cancer though. Some of us will die of old age before the cancer gets us. We'll have heart attacks or whatever. But when a child *has* cancer and an adult *has* cancer and they come into the hospital, and they're thinking about dying, well, they're *not* dying then. You may be when you're relapsed on all the available treatments and your cancer is growing and you've developed a pneumonia that is resistant to antibiotics or it can't be treated. When you come into the hospital not breathing, well, maybe you're dying then. But it's possible to be honest with people and to give them some information.

Remember the classic line in the movies: "How many months have I got?" Those kinds of questions you can't really answer, because you're damned if you do and you're damned if you don't. You tell them they have six months and they live seven months; they're mad at you. You tell them they've got six months and they die in five; they're furious. So you can tell people, "I don't think you're dying now because you have something that we can treat. Yes, cystic fibrosis is a terminal illness as best we know today, but you don't look that sick to me right now, and I think we have antibiotics that we can use," and so forth. And when the patient actually is dying, when that final hospital admission or episode at home comes, they'll know, because they will feel weaker.

Just to answer that last question in closing notes, concerning the dream and the vision the youngster had, I continue to be amazed at the imponderables that science cannot define. And obviously we don't know where that idea got into the little girl's head. But I have seen patients who no one expected to die come into the hospital and die. We had a young man last week who told his parents he had to come to the hospital. A nineteen-year-old man with cystic fibrosis. And they drove two hours back into the hospital, and he came to the hospital and got admitted. During the admitting process he said he was feeling very sick, and he didn't want to die at home because he didn't think his parents could handle that. Got admitted. Brought him up. Laid down in the bed. Said to someone, "Am I here?" And they said, "Yes." And he died. Accounting for those kinds of experiences is something that human beings have not gotten to the point of defining scientifically.

But there was another study which I will say in closing which is the icing on the cake—some of the studies of people who die relative to their birthdays or important life events. If you're going to die within a month of some significant life event such as your birthday, your wedding anniversary, Christmas, Easter, if those are important days for you, then you're more likely to die in the period after the holiday than in the period before it. Why is that? How? What enables people to hold on for that extra period of time? That's one of the imponderables.

Question: I just wanted to ask you since you have centered on presenting death of children, how can you tell a grown-up like you or me, from your psychological point of view, how can you present death? How are you going to tell me in a more comfortable way?

Dr. Koocher: I don't know that I would have much to tell you about how to cope with it or about what death is. When people ask me I say that I don't know. I'm sure we all have our fantasies about what death is like. I guess what I would say is, it's important for you to know that you have some condition that seems like it's going to prove terminal. Then say, "Look, this is what's the matter with you. It's treatable or it's not treatable. You keep advised at every step of the way about your own condition. And if the condition is such that it's not going to be treatable, it's going to result in death; I think it's important to tell you.

I don't have to tell you about the ancient Greek tradition of killing the bearer of bad news on certain occasions—and no one wants to be the bearer of news like that. But not to tell a person is to rob them of something very important—to rob them of the right to make what peace they need to make to deal with things that they need to deal with. The person may choose not to deal with them, to deny it or avoid it, but that's the indivdual's decision. And the most difficult part about it is overcoming the emotional barrier of not wanting to be the person to tell you this terrible thing. But as I said, people generally do not fall apart. I will go so far as to say I have never seen someone have a "nervous breakdown." In fact, I've seen some people who were very troubled, emotionally, prior to ever getting a terminal illness, who were able to pull themselves together and cope with their psychiatric illness because they knew they'd have less time and they had something with which they had to deal.

Chapter Four

DEATH AND DYING: PASTORAL-PSYCHOLOGICAL PERSPECTIVE

Earl Grollman

Let me begin with the word that's part of my tradition, and it's also part of your tradition. It's the word in Hebrew for hello and goodbye and peace. What's the word?

Audience: Shalom!

Rabbi Grollman: People often ask the question, why do the Jewish people have the same word for hello and goodbye. Because in my congregation in Belmont they don't know whether they're coming or going— I always make sure I'm a few miles away when I say that.

One person said, "You are a Rabbi—I want to know what are the Jewish views?" Well, before anybody asks me any further questions like this, let me tell you that the only similarity that one Jew has in common with the second Jew is the agreement that the third Jew should give to charity! So there is no unanimity.

Wherever I go, I'm always asked the same question, and this is really the topic in terms of a psychological approach which is also pastoral: how did you get involved in this whole field of death and dying? The answer is really very simple. Whenever you need a communication expert, it's a person who doesn't know how to talk, right? Whenever you hear a minister speak against materialism, he's going to ask for an increase in salary. So I write about those subjects that I *really* can't handle. I write a book to answer the questions, and after I write the book, it's the wrong answer. But a person's reach should exceed the grasp or what's a heaven for?

I'm the most unlikely person to talk about the subject, because I come from a family where the word death was never mentioned.

45

It was a dirty word. I remember once being at a family gathering where my grandmother said, "When I die—" It was natural. She was in her eighties. And my uncle, who was the head of the Psychology Department at John Hopkins University said, "Don't say it. Don't say that word." And he never said it. My Grandmother died but I wasn't allowed to go to the funeral because I was "too young." I was fourteen-years-old. I was the intercollegiate wrestling champion of the State of Maryland, but that has nothing to do with towers. My mother and father said "Earl, you really don't want to go to the funeral, *do you*? And I did not go.

In order to be ordained a Rabbi in my denomination, after four years of college we have an additional six years of seminary because we have so much more to teach. In my seminary, as in most seminaries until recently, there was never a discussion of death or dying. We had courses in theology, courses in "Is there life after life?" We had courses in liturgy, what kind of prayers to be taught; we had courses in homeletics, what kind of eulogy to be delivered; but nothing about what happens when real people die. I was ordained in Boston as an assistant. It doesn't make any difference if you're Greek Orthodox or whatever, when the assistant minister comes to town, that very day the senior minister goes on vacation.

I was sitting in my little office a couple of weeks later and the telephone rang and someone said, "Rabbi Grollman?" I said, "Yes?"—very gruff because I thought that's the way Rabbis should sound. And the person said, "Something terrible has happened. Our twelve-year-old son had just drowned at his summer camp." It was my first confrontation with death, the first time I had ever been in a funeral home, the first time I had ever seen a dead body. And I was expected to give solace and comfort and consolation. I had no idea what I was doing.

The years have gone by and because I am a clergy person, it's part of my life—the most difficult part of my life—given that I can go from wedding to funeral, wedding to funeral, and at the end of that day, I am literally wiped out. Someday, there should be a discussion on who takes care of the care-giver. I didn't know what I was doing. But I was handling it.

Then my closest friend was sick. They said it was psychosomatic, which meant the doctor didn't know. And the day that he was to see the psychologist, he died. I came to the home on a Sunday night from the Mount Auburn Hospital in Cambridge. I walked into the house and the children did not say, "Rabbi Grollman" or "Doctor

Grollman" which makes me feel even better. They said, "Uncle Earl, what will we do?" And I'm not going to be cutesy and say, "There's nothing wrong with being a coward." We don't always say everything we mean and mean everything we say. Had it happened that way, I would not be in my congregation thirty-two days. I've been there thirty-two years.

When somebody says, "How do you like this picture?" What are you going to say? It is terrible? I always say, "Interesting." You know, we don't always say what we mean. And the children said, "What will we do?" And I thought, all I have to do is go to the Widener Library, which is close enough (I am in Belmont) and take out a book on what to say to children. Would you believe, in the 1960's, not one, single, solitary volume on what to say to children?

The day of the funeral, as I was about to leave, the telephone rang. It's a name known to many of you in the field of mental health, a Dr. Gerald Kaplan of the Havard Divinity School. At that time, living under the influence of Freud and also in the book dealing with logotherapy and existentialism and Victor Frankel, very theoretically, he said, "I know you're interested in the field of death in psychology. Would you be interested in working in the field of death? We have a bereavement team." And I said, " If you had called me two days ago, I would not have any interest."

Until this, I had never expeditioned into the field of dying and death. And what I learned is something I should have known from the very beginning that the word "dead"—d-e-a-d, is merely the four letter word of pornography. It's the one word that is seldom, if ever, discussed in plain language. Most often, in theology seminaries, we discuss it in theological terms. Too often we suffer paralysis to intellectual analysis. We don't talk about it. We don't share our feelings because we give a quotation from the Bible and say, "This is why I went to this seminary."

And reality got through to us in the study that we made when a hundred and fifty widows were asked, "Who helped with the time of death?" Only one person said, "The Clergy." Only one! No one said, "The physician." Many said, "The nurses"—who are the real heroines. Strangely enough, the people who rated the highest outside of support groups and friends, the highest were at the funeral practice—the funeral directors. You know why? *Because they were there!* As clergy, we've gone in and said our prayers because we're intimidated by death—many of us are.

If there's one book you should read, it's not my book. It's by

Margaret Tita Bowers. It's called *The Conflicts of the Clergy* and why we become clergy in the first place. Because we want to conquer death. We go in, we have a theological and religious orientation, and there's nothing wrong with that. That's why we are here at school. But we fail to understand where people are. I became interested in children and death for a very specific reason. Because in many cases when the child comes back, wherever he or she may be, he's lost into a house full of people. In any case, there's an almost failure to say your mother has died. Your father has died. Your grandparent has died. The adults say, "I can't handle it. How can my poor children understand what's happening?"

And since there are many clergy, we walk in and speak to the adults—but the kids are all by themselves crying their eyes out. I became interested in children for almost a selfish reason. I had been reading Emerson's journal and make the depicted statement that when it comes to death, each one of us is a child in his words. So, if I talk about children, I'm not talking about your sons or your daughters or your grandchildren. Each one of us is a child when it comes to dying and death. And children will understand it at different developmental levels.

To the very small child, death is de-personal. Did you ever play cops and robbers when you were growing up? Didn't you go, "Bang! I shot you. You're dead. Okay. Now that you're dead, let's play another game." Am I making myself clear? You're dead but you're not dead. Many things that children play are death-oriented games. Ring Around the Rosy. London Bridges Falling Down. You're dead but you're not dead.

Natalie Wood dies. You can rest assured that on Channel 56, for the next three weeks, you will see reruns of Natalie Wood movies. "I thought she died." "She didn't die, dear." "She did!" They see a dead bird on the ground and an identical bird flying overhead. So what happens? The bird flies away. They think that death is very often the next holiday that's coming—Halloween. Death is an anthropomorphism, a theological term. Death is a person, and the way he will die is to be killed, because that's how they see that. Before a young person reaches the age of fifteen, that person has seen approximately seventeen thousand deaths on television. And almost always there are killings and murders. This is why you might say to a young child, "Your grandfather has died," and the child would say, "Who deaded him?" Because death for them is often in terms of being killed or murdered. And that's the headlines that they see in *The Boson Globe.*

As they grow older, they understand people will die but they won't die. Then they reach a certain age and they understand that the "law of death" governs us all. That's what it says. I don't believe it.

In the next three weeks I will be in seven different hospices all over the country. This coming Monday, in Indiana; and Tuesday, in Chicago. And we know that so often, after a long, lingering illness and you're working with a family, you walk in and you say, "Well, who is the king over there? Where is the senator? Where are the important papers?" Thinking the primitive thoughts of children. They think if you buy a cemetery plot while the person is dying, this will precipitate and expedite the person's death.

We don't even use the right words. There are all kinds of euphemisms and circumlocutions that we use because we can't handle death. So what do we do when a person dies? What are the words? "Passed away." What does that mean? My kids did well in school in June. What happens? They pass. They didn't "pass away." "Pass on." If you work in the medical facility, what's the word? Expire. Elizabeth Kübler-Ross, a close friend of mine, who spoke in the afternoon to a student with whom she worked at a six-hundred bed facility, said, "I'd like to work with some dying people. The adminstrator says, "In our hospital, nobody dies. They expire." Physicians are there to sustain life, and when death occurs they feel in some way responsible. So, they deal with death by taking out the word God or death.

These are the words children understand. When we "lost him." He said, "Who's being lost?" I'm always losing my keys; so if you lose something you find it." "But the reason why she died was because she was so good, so loving." Do you ever hear that? "God loved her. God picks the prettiest flowers." It's a lie. In your Bible and in my Bible there's a book called the Book of Job. Three people came to Job and said, "The reason why we feel the slings and arrows of outrageous fortune are that you must have done something wrong." And Job said, "I don't believe that." That's the Jewish-Christian approach. Forget that.

There's a movie that keeps reoccurring called, "Yours, Mine and Ours" with Lucille Ball. I don't know the other actors it has. Remember Lucille Ball plays the part of the widow. Her husband had just died. And John—is acting up all over the place. She comes and she says, "Why are you being that way? Why are you acting that way?" And little Johnny replies, "Because you said God takes

those who are good. I don't want God to take me." The corollary
to that is if God takes those who are good, then what are you doing
here? I think it would make me a potential atheist to believe that
God would reward me by taking me before my allotted time. Just
because you go to church, you will live longer? If this were so, there
would be an addition to every church and every synagogue.

I think you can be careful with a lot of things that we say in terms
of religion—that we believe in heaven—and I think we have to share
it with people around us. Children don't understand what you're
talking about. "What does it mean to be up in Heaven?" If you
really want to talk to children, you can go through the psychoanalytic literature. You'll hear, "If your mother's up in Heaven, why are
we putting her in the ground? How does she get up there?" From
the magical literature, you know that children who are in an airplane
look through the windows: they are looking to see the person who
is God. Or it's raining and their eyes are transfixed, waiting for the
person to come down. "I think he disappeared." Look at the words
that we are using. Whether we are hospice workers or social workers
or whatever; this is all nomenclature that becomes part of our language and confuses everybody else. One expression that causes so
much consternation—and it comes from the animal kingdom: we
take the dog or cat to the vet and the vet says, "There's nothing
more we can do." So what do you do? You put the animal "to
sleep." But we know that there are many children who are afraid
to go to bed at night because for them death and sleep are synono-
mous. Can you imagine the pathological dread of going to bed at
night after a member sibling had died of sudden infant death syndrome in his or her sleep? And some funeral directors have rooms
in their mortuary which they call "The Slumber Room."

I spoke before a group of funeral directors. I said, "I don't like
the words 'Slumber Room'." Someone said, "I'm not going to call
it a dead room just to be understood." Another said, "What room
would you call it?" And being a rabbi, I said. "How about shalom?
It means hello, good-bye, it means peace." "Sorry," said a member
of the Missouri Synod, this will never do!" So then, after that I said,
"And what would you call it?" He said, "How about 'Rest Room'."

What I'm trying to say is words have different meanings for different roles. I was a member of one of the earliert interfaith movements. Thirty-two years ago, Cardinal Cushing was president and
we met together for a year. Most of us were born in this country
and had earned advanced degrees. But if I say the word salvation

and you use the word salvation, Father, we're talking about different things. I used the Hebrew "gashima" which had a different meaning, and finally someone said, "We better define our terms." Because when we talk to people, we may know where *we* are, but we have no idea where *they* are. And I'll never forget when I was working on a book and I was meeting with a group of children. One kid said, "How long is death? And I said, "Death is permanent." He said, "That's wonderful! That's great!" "What do you mean it's wonderful?" I asked. He said, "All I know is my mother has a permanent." "So what happens?" "You come back six months later?"

I think it's important that when we deal with people who are going through crisis, you hear what's being said. You need to go over and over and over it again. And when you come in and we give all the "carcinoma" language remember that we usually do this in ignorance to show how smart we are. It is not understanding. It's like the anniversary coming in November when President Kennedy was assassinated. Tell me exactly what you were doing the moment you heard President Kennedy was assassinated.

Man: I was watching television.

Rabbi: You were watching television. Where were you, Father? What were you doing?

Clergyman: I was in a car going to a hospital.

I could go to every single person in here and each person would remember. It would be like a bookmark in a diary. And with most of us it came back, that Friday afternoon. I was doing doctoral studies at Boston University School of Theology at that time. I was in the Dugout having a beer. We walked across the street and someone said, "My God, he's shot!" I didn't know whether he was dead or not. At that moment, they didn't know. And the thing is, I watched the same television programs as you did, again and again and again. Because you don't walk in and say, "I already told you," you have to hear it again and again and again.

And the question is, as in a pastoral-psychological way, how do you help people? I think we help people not by telling them how they ought to feel. You don't know how pain is going to feel. I think like a good physician, as you are, when you give a prescription, you say, "Now these are some of the side effects. You might feel a little woozy and your throat may be dry." And if you feel that way, say, "Hey, I know this is the way I'm supposed to feel; it doesn't make me feel unnatural. It's the way most people feel who are going through the bereavement process." They'll say, "I'm going crazy.

I'm losing my mind. I can't eat, I can't sleep, I can't concentrate.
I'm driving my car and I come to a stoplight. I can't remember
whether it means to stop or to go. I call someone on the telephone.
I forgot who I'm calling. Am I losing my mind?''

What I like to do when I walk in is to sit on the floor with the
children and adults who are sitting around on the couch and the sofa.
Because when I'm on the same level with the children, they can talk
to me. If I stand over them, then I'm ninety feet tall, symbolically,
as a clergy person. And I'll say, I don't know how you're going to
feel, but this is the way you may be feeling. You almost feel like
you're in shock. You don't even hear what you're saying. You feel
like you're numb. But your power block is that you're like a spec-
tator. And all of a sudden you say, *"My God, am I scared."* You
want to believe that it's a nightmare—that it didn't happen and you'd
wake up and you'd find that it didn't happen. It's like John-John,
President Kennedy's son, returning to Washington six months after
his father's assassination and asking the secretary, *"Where is my
father?"* Sounds like a little child, right? We're all children. All of
us who have been through a death in our own families.

The telephone rings days and weeks and months later: "Maybe
it's my father?" You hear footsteps in the house: "Look who's
here!" We see the mind understands. The body refuses to accept
it. It's not only because the funeral is over. It's just beginning. The
most difficult time for any widow is not at the time of death. It's
six to nine months later when the tumult and shock die and everybody
else has gone away and they're left alone and bereft. And nobody
cares, especially your clergy. No one cares. I believe that it did not
happen. And I'll meet the people and they'll say, "You know it's
worse today than it was nine months ago." And she said, "Should
it be that way?" "Of course it should be that way. Your bodies don't
feel well. They're not functioning the way that they should because
whatever happens to your mind if you're in pain and anguish has
to affect the way you feel. Unfortunately, many people go to the
physician and will get tranquilizer after tranquilizer and there becomes this chemical dependency.

There's a new study at the University of Southern Illinois that
says we should take no more than one mild tranquilizer every third
day. Sure, it's painful. But short-range pain equals long-range gain.
And they have to go through this pain and you can't camouflage
it. For some of the people who are going through this pain, they
feel guilt that they can't handle the guilt, so they project the guilt.

And some of the people whom they will hate will be the clergyman, the doctor, the psychologist. As the surrogate of God, how could you allow this to happen? They may be angry at God, and that's okay. God can take it.

This morning at my synagogue we read this section of Sodom and Gammorah where Abraham dares to say to God, and I love it: "Shall not the God of Justice do justly? "Cursed be the day that I was born—the Book of Job—and in your faith: "My God, my God, why have you forsaken me?" Where can I turn? We don't want to accept responsibility. And so we try to fault—I can blame the doctor, the nurse; what am I saying? Don't blame me!

And in my book on suicide we found that in almost every suicide there is someone who is held accountable, usually the most caring, giving person, but the one least able to defend himself. So if I said, "You killed him," I'm saying, "Please don't blame me." Because many of us do feel guilt. We replay the ninth inning. "If only I had called the doctor sooner." "If only I were more loving." "If only I were more caring." If only . . . if only . . . if only." Because we're all children: when we are good, we are rewarded; and when we are bad, we are punished."

Four hundred and ninety-some persons were incinerated in the Coconut Grove fire. A psychiatrist, Dr. Lindemann, went to the individual homes and kept hearing the same statement. "I had a fight with my boyfriend; that's why I'm being punished," And as a clergyperson, we hear people say, "Father, why am I being punished? Is it death? Is it the bottom of chastisement?" I say to people, "I cannot stop you from suffering. You have a good reason to suffer. Your mother has died." "Your father has died." "Your child has died." And every death is different. If it's the death of a child, it is the death of a future. If it's the death of a parent it is the death of the past. If there's the death of a spouse, there is the death of the present (see Appendix 1). I cannot stop them from suffering. But I can stop you from suffering for the wrong reasons and this is much of the source of guilt people allocate to themselves. You and I both have the resource of forgiveness. And I will say to people, "I believe that God forgives." That's what we're facing with death. The question is, if God forgives, will you learn to forgive yourself? How do we help people? By allowing them to participate in the rite of passage, by allowing them to say good-bye—and children should be permitted to say good-bye as well as adults. We always explain in advance what's happening. They have to know what's happening, "You know we're going to the church. There will be the priest, Father So-and-So." There's a cast. The secret is out. Anything which is mentionable is manageable.

But how many or us as clergy don't talk to people? How many of us share their feelings, whatever they need to feel? And this is the best audio-visual aid I know—it's the ability to go in and say, "We are saying good-bye. Now you know where your father is." There are no secrets. And if you want to cry, you can cry." I've been with a group of priests and ministers in Israel. We went by a place called the "Church of the Tears," where Jesus wept for Lazarus, and yet, I have heard clergy people say faith and tears don't mix! Of course, when this one dies, part of us has died. The first time I ever cried in front of my congregation, I thought I had destroyed them, and then I learned that they were going around crying, saying it's okay for us to cry. And it hurts to say good-bye. And it doesn't even insure religious faith because the funeral is both the celebration of the life that was lived and it commemorates the fact that on this earthly pilgrimage you have your own religious resources. We are not going to see that person again. We don't have that much time—and as a clergyperson, I want to tell you I have no answers.

The time I fail people is when I write a book. Because I'm not listening. I think the way that I help people is to listen and to be close to them and to sit. Then something will happen. I will walk in and I will touch them. My parents taught me this. You can touch people. People know when. We were talking about communication— I look into your eyes—that's hard for clergypeople, because it's easier to say a prayer. It's the sitting when they have a dead one—to look into their eyes and to hold their hand. I do not walk in and say, "I know exactly how you feel." I don't hold anybody's hand except my own. I don't walk in and say, "Isn't it wonderful she lived to a ripe old age."

My mother died last year. It was terrible. Painfully, I wrote about it. When it happens to me it is the worst tragedy in the world. And when people said, "Isn't it nice she lived to a ripe old age," it denied me the opportunity to grieve. I don't want to walk in and say, "It's God's will." You are not privy to that information. I remember someone walking in and saying,"It's all for the best." "What do you mean it's for the best?"

I remember a young person whose husband had died. At the cemetary somebody came over to her and said, "You are young.

You are so pretty. You will be married in no time.'' From a pastoral point of view, the highest theology is to be there. The highest theology is to sit next to the person, and not at the time of death. That's expected. But to call later. Write down the date that the person died. And just say, ''I am thinking of you.'' They never forget. You can give the greatest sermon in the world but the fact that you act is their due. It shows that you care! That you are involved! That it's possible.

Instead of people coming to my office or my coming to their home, I take them out. We go to ''Fantasia,'' and sit down and we have a martini and we talk. And we share. While they're telling how they're really feeling, all that I can say is somebody is there. And the whole approach, to be with people, is your theology, which you have but more important is your presence. And this is what they will remember. You are there. Not to tell them but to listen. And if they're angry at God, let them be angry at God. It's what Sigmund Freud calls the ties of dissolution; when you're able to talk, the better they are able to work it through. None of this idealization with your eulogies.

We have people that would never remarry after their husband's death even if the dead spouse were to return. Somebody once said there's no such thing as a perfect individual. A man said, ''Yes, there is—my wife's first husband that died.''

I will say to people, unless you can understand what that person was not as well as what that person *is and was*, you're not working yourself through the bereavement process. What it means in terms of a pastoral approach is through theology. We each worship. That's important. There can be new approaches in that worship service. It doesn't always have to be the same. It's not a xerox. Everything always the same as every other thing. My mother was different from your mother.

And I'll end with two stories. One is the story of an old Hassidic rabbi who said to his disciple, ''Do you know what gives me pain?'' And the youngster said, ''How do I know what gives you pain, Rabbi?'' And the old man said, ''If you do not know what gives me pain, you really don't love me.'' So in the eyes of God there is nothing you can say that He didn't already know. This shows how important it is to be there and to care and to share.

And, finally, the story of Martin Luther who was worshiping one evening. Somebody knocked on the door and said, ''Can I see you, Dr. Luther?'' Dr. Luther said, ''I can't see you now. It's my evening prayer.'' And Martin Luther wrote, ''I never saw that person again. He committed suicide. Here I had a chance to be with God, and I lost God—in prayer.'' Seek God in prayer—but be there!

That's how we show how much we care, by understanding the people who we are with when they are in pain. Shalom!

Question: I very much enjoyed your talk and I wanted to hear more about your thoughts about forgiveness and what that really entails.

Rabbi Grollman: First of all, when we deal with people of all ages, we have to understand that many of the things which they're asking for, concerning forgiveness, they don't need. I went to speak in Chicago about Sudden Infant Death Syndrome many years ago and the talk was recorded by the organizer's son. I spoke about how older children felt when younger siblings die. They hear so many times, "Isn't it wonderful; isn't she beautiful." They feel, "Nobody's paying any attention to me." And so the infant dies and the older child thinks that the wish is causative. The child thinks that he caused the death of the younger sibling. It makes sense to me. I know of a mother and her son. They were driving back to their home. And the young man said to his mother, "All of these years I thought I killed my sister because I was so jealous." I think we have to say— all of us say things we shouldn't say. All of us do things we shouldn't do. That's what makes us human.

We need to understand where people are—and to be able to separate and to set a line of demarcation. And then to say, okay you did a dirty thing, right? You're not God. You're finite. You're not infinite. But the whole idea is how can you make noble ignoble misfortune? The people who are working in hospice and acting as friends and candlelighters. Do we have any of these groups here today? They're taking their own pain and they're helping other people to work it through. And every time I get, "What kind of work do you do?" Every time you help somebody else, you're helping yourself. Last Wednesday I spoke at Ann Arbor before the Pediatric Oncology Social Workers. And the strange part was throughout the whole day of discussion, nobody talked about their clients. They talked about their own fields. And that's a real problem. We get involved but we forget that we're real human beings as well. So I think the whole issue is, first, to understand where people are rather than to come in directively and say this is what you should do and we quote from the Bible.

Question: I worked in a school where there was a suicide last year. That issue, I think, has never been resolved. Can you give us suggestions?

people I love being with the most are younger people, because, you know, it's not a question of whether you're going to have death education. The question is whether that's going to be a good death education. And children don't have that from their church except in religious tones which they don't quite understand. And so as a result, they really don't know what is going on. I went to speak at a school not more than ten miles from here where a physical education teacher had been killed. And the teachers had a petition that I not be allowed to talk to the kids. Because they said, "Look, he's been dead for over a month." I did not know that this person who had died had a wife who was a teacher and she stood up and said, "All of the teachers here pretend that my husband never lived. And I need to talk. But the kids have been great." So where I will spend a lot of time is talking with children. And you don't have to wait until somebody dies. I don't think I would say, "Today we're going to talk about suicide." I think I would talk. I wouldn't say, "Today we're going to talk about suicide because first of all, suicide is the second killer of young people. The first is accidents and many accidents are really suicides."

I went to a community in Wennetka, Illinois, where an eleven-year-old girl had committed suicide. I spoke to the staff, the teachers and the Wennetkans said, "We're the best school system in the country. It shouldn't have even happened to us." Many of them felt guilty that they didn't pick it up. I spoke to the students and somebody said, "I yelled at that person before that person went." The girl had committed suicide by hanging herself. The kids were afraid to go into their closets the next day, thinking that somebody was taking his or her life. So I think one way of doing it is allowing children to get rid of their feelings. Maybe they didn't like this person. And that's okay.

So I would think that what you should be doing is what they're doing in school systems all over the country. We're bringing death out of the closet. It's a reality. It's happening. Let's talk about reality. Now let's talk about it and how do you feel.

Appendix 1

HANDLING DIFFICULT GRIEF CRISES

Each death is different. When a parent dies, one loses the past. When a spouse dies, one loses the future. Even though grief is a common human experience,it is as individual as fingerprints—it shows itself in widely differing ways.

The following are some guidelines for the sorts of death experience that are encountered infrequently—where information may be scant. To be effective, we must be aware of all kinds of loss, the frequent as well as the less common incidences of death: loss of a newborn, sudden infant death, a death that was unanticipated, suicide, and special feelings of the clergy person—so well acquainted with grief—when a loved one of his own has died. There are sources of help to assist the bereaved in coping with grief and loneliness and provide for continuing reassurance and understanding. People differ more widely in their reactions to death than they do to any other human experience. There is no magical procedure that will comfort all people, either at the time of death or during the period that follows.

The problem is not that the clergy person will not always succeed in grief counseling. The tragedy is that the clergy person may not be well-informed and at least attempt to do his or her best to help people in times of crisis. As Mark Twain said: "It's not what people know that gets them into trouble; but it's what they know that isn't so."

People differ more widely in their reaction to death than to any other human experience. While bereavement and grief are the most universal of all human experiences—and the most human—they are also the most painful. Information is not adequate if it remains with the clergy person *alone*. Those insights must be shared in a non-threatening way to help make the agonizing period less stressful and less frightening. Then survivors will not be caught unaware and

58

unprepared for their often bizarre but rarely spoken sensations, thoughts and behavioral changes. They need to understand that these changes are normal in the face of the very unusual and traumatic death in their family. And don't forget: just being with the bereaved is often more important than what you say.

LIVING WITH NEWBORN DEATH

How often do newborns die?

Within the first 28 days of life, approximately 35,000 newborn infants die in this country every year. In addition, 33,000 fetal deaths or stillbirths occur after the 20th week of pregnancy. Taken together, these 68,000 deaths add up to one death every seven minutes. The cold statistic translates into an enormous collection of human suffering for surviving parents, siblings and the greater circle of family and friends. A child's death is no longer in the ordinary order of events. We expect older people to die—but not young babies. It doesn't seem fair that they die before they have a chance to live.

What about stillbirths?

Stillbirths occur in about one in 80 deliveries. After the birth and death, there is usually a conspiracy of silence. Parents are rarely encouraged to see and touch the dead body. Frequently, the baby is not given a name and the mother is quickly discharged—as if nothing had occurred. Rituals and rites of passage are seldom offered. The funeral (if there is one) is often private, without the mother and sometimes without the father being present. Most health professionals do little or no follow-up. Stillbirth is a non-event. It is as if the mother never carried her child. As if the father had no hopes and aspirations. There is no communication about the misery, the guilt, the shame, the failure.

What can the clergy person do in this tragic climate?

First, help the family to face reality. The child is dead. And no matter how brief the life, there are deep emotional attachments. The parents desperately need to cope and to respond to their loss. How hard it is to grieve the death of a dream! Help the family make their baby—and their loss—more real with something tangible to hold on to—a hospital bracelet, a lock of hair, photographs, birth and death notices. These reminders dramatize the fact that a profound event indeed touched their lives—ever so swiftly. Let parents mourn a reality, not an illusion.

If the parents desire, let them view and touch their dead child. Too often the infant is rushed from the mother to a special (care) unit—never to be seen again. Many parents who have had the opportunity to hold their child have remarked how therapeutic this touching has been. "Now I know my child lived. I am better able to accept that he died." This is true even when the infant is physically deformed. Beauty is in the eyes of the beholder.

As options are offered to the family, describe in advance the child's appearance. Explain that the body is cold. We may offer our support by saying, "If you want, I'll stay with you. Tell me what's best for you." Understand that funerals are not solely for people who have lived a long while. The importance of funeral rituals for infant deaths had been emphasized by Dr. D. Gary Benfield, Director of the Regional Neonatal Intensive Care Unit, Children's Hospital Medical Center of Akron and Hane A. Nichols, Bereavement Consultant. They afford both closure and relief.

SUDDEN INFANT DEATH SYNDROME (CRIB DEATH)

Is there a typical history?

There is no classical case. Both rich and poor, white, black and yellow are the victims. SIDS is not preventable nor predictable. The infant is usually put to bed after a feeding without any suspicion that something is out of the ordinary. Sometime later, a few minutes, several hours or the following morning, whenever the parents next check on the baby, the infant is found lifeless. There is no outcry, no struggle. The infant may be lying face up or face down in the crib. Occasionally, there is a pinkish froth coming from the nose, or a spot of blood on the bed. The face and remainder of the body may bear bluish-purple discolorations which may appear to be bruises. These are normal post-mortem changes and should not be mistaken for injuries.

What are some of the reactions of the parents?

"What did I do wrong?" "Was it my fault?" "Why didn't I

detect that there was something wrong with my child?''

Lola Redford, wife of actor Robert Redford, tells how guilty they both felt after their firstborn died in his crib. ''I had this notion that when you come from strong Mormon stock, you just don't have children who die.'' She also spoke of not being willing to hire a baby-sitter for her two subsequent children, of spending all her energy ''guarding'' them. ''For almost nine years, I gave those children my undivided 100 percent neurotic attention. I was so afraid they would die.''

How about the Grandparents?

Grandparents are often unaware of the mysterious, sudden, un-expected death called SIDS. They may believe that the tragedy could have been averted by some action of their children such as a more proper diet or closer observation during a virus. Worst of all, they may believe the baby died because of some omission or neglect. Grandparents need continual reassurance that the cause of the di-sease remains unknown and that the parents did not cause nor could they have prevented this crashing, bitter disappointment.

Grandparents often take charge of the funeral arrangements. After all, they are older and more experienced in the sad prepara-tion for death. The clergyperson might do well to say: ''I know you are going through an ordeal. But you know, of course, that your children are the ones who feel the loss most keenly. Perhaps it would be better for your children to come to their own decisions about what is best for *them*!''

What can the clergy person do to help the family?

Tell them that SIDS occurs in apparently healthy, normal, thriv-ing babies who have received the most skillful and loving care. The death does not reflect *in any way* on the ability of the parents to care for their children. SIDS is not suffocation or pneumonia. They did nothing to cause the death.

Should there be an autopsy?

Usually the examination reveals no disease sufficient to account for death. In approximately fifteen percent of the cases, how-ever, post-mortem examination exposes a previously unsuspected abnormality or rapidly fatal infectious disease. This is one of the reasons autopsy on these infants is so important.

Did my child suffer?

Explain to the family that evidence underscores the point that the infant was *not* in pain. In most cases, death is sudden, almost instantaneous. There are examples when the child "just stopped breathing" in the arms of the parent. The adults report a sense of peacefulness and quietude.

DEATH BY SUICIDE

What is the incidence of suicide?

Once every minute, someone attempts to kill himself or herself with conscious intent. Sixty or seventy times a day these attempts succeed. In America, the problem has reached somewhere between twenty-two and twenty-five thousand annually or one suicide every twenty-six minutes.

Who would destroy something so precious as life?

Almost everybody at one time or another contemplates suicide. Death is one of the chioces open to human beings. Suicide has been known in all times and committed by all manner of people, from Saul, Sappho and Seneca to Virginia Woolf, James Forrestall, Marilyn Monroe and Earnest Hemingway. Every person is a potential suicide.

How is suicide different from other deaths?

Of course, natural death has its share of emotional overtones: loneliness, disbelief, heartache and torment. With self-inflicted death, the emotions are *intensified* to unbelievable and unbearable proportions. Those left behind experience not only pain of separation but aggravated feelings of guilt, shame and self-blame.

The act of self-destruction raises the obvious questions, "Why?" and "What could I have done to prevent it?" Anxious and grief-stricken, the survivors ask, "How can I face my friends? What will they think of me?" Death by suicide is the greatest of all affronts to those who remain. Special counseling skills are needed to cope with the runaway emotions of the bereaved. Suicide stigmatizes not only the victim but the survivors as well.

Shouldn't the funeral be private?

It is understandable that when the survivors hear the shocking news their first impulse is to hold the funeral as quickly as possible. After all, there is an aura of shame and dishonor. As a result, a private service may be contemplated for the immediate family only.

However, no matter how great the humiliation the relatives cannot hide from the bitter truth. No one can run away from pain. A private funeral seems to say that because the family is unable to bear the disgrace they want to keep it "secret." The mourners overlook one important fact: when given the opportunity, friends can be of inestimable value. The funeral, where no one is invited but all may attend, affords a sharing occasion for supportive love at a time when it is so desperately needed. One person is no person. The solitary heart must throb with the caring heart of others.

How about self-help groups?

Many people who themselves have experienced the death of a loved one have developed tremendous gifts of insight. They understand the value of sharing. They may help the bereaved to reach out of their isolation to an important support system. Fellow sufferers often become second families to each other. Some helpful organizations include:

Candlelighters, 123 C Street, Southeast, Washington D.C. 20003. This is an international organization of parents whose children have cancer or died from this disease.

Compassionate Friends. P.O. Box 1347, Oak Brook, Illinois 60521. A support group for bereaved parents who "need not walk alone."

Sudden Infant Death Syndrome Foundation, 1501 Broadway, New York, New York 10036. The group intervenes on behalf of stricken parents of SIDS or "crib death" with professional counseling services for adult and children.

Widowed-to-Widowed Program. Begun at the Laboratory of
Community Psychiatry, Harvard Medical School, 58 Feinwood
Rd., Boston, Massachusetts 02115. There are hundreds of these
organizations throughout the United States. They bring together
the widow and widower in fellowship and help them find a new
way of life.

Parents Without Partners, 7910 Woodmont Avenue. Washington, D.C. 20014. A non-sectarian organization with a member-
ship of a hundred thousand in over 700 chapters concerned with
the welfare of single parents and their children. It assures them
that they are not alone. Their motto is "Sharing by Caring."
If such an organization does not exist in your area, the clergy
person could be instrumental in its formation.

Chapter Five

DEATH AND DYING:
THEOLOGICAL PERSPECTIVES

Thomas Hopko

It's awesome to have to be presenting late today, especially after what we've heard—particularly being a pastor or a priest in a School of Theology and a professor of theology. But I do think that what I have to say, although it will be perhaps more abstract as a presentation than the speakers who went before me, will be basically within the same perspective of the same concerns, and perhaps even, hopefully, provide a theological vision at least for Eastern Orthodox Christians, on the issues of death and dying.

I realize that when we speak about a theological perspective it means a very particular theological perspective. If I were a Buddhist, I would give one theological perspective about the death experience. Likewise, if I were a Moslem or if I were one of another type of Christian; and as the Rabbi said, there are many kinds of Jewish opinions as well. And as a matter of fact, even within the Orthodox Church there are many Christian opinions, particularly when it comes to death.

My own opinion is that of having at least being able to speak from the ink, from the books, from the writings, the Bible, the Church Fathers, the liturgies, the saints. My opinion is and I would dare to say that, statistically, most members of the Orthodox Church including the clergy, are presenting a theology of death which is much more a combination of modern American attitudes and some form of Platonism than they are presenting the vision of death that is given in the Bible and certainly that is presented in the Gospel concerning Jesus Christ.

Instead of listening to theological points, I'd just like to begin with two stories, both of which I should dare to say are from my own life. For, even though I'm known as a professor of theology,

I still work in a church in New York City. I'm not a pastor anymore after twenty years. Finally, I just couldn't handle everything so I ceased being the pastor of the church on Pentecost Sunday. So right now I am wandering but I'd like to make my theological points first in two stories from my own pastoral experience and then perhaps go into what might be called creative abstractions.

When I was first ordained and sent to a church in Ohio, of course, we had funerals. It was one of those ethnic communities—a Russian neighborhood parish. I would drive around with the funeral director, talking with one of these men and he said, "You know, Father Hopko, I've been a funeral director all my life. My father was a funeral director in this town. My wife's father was a funeral director in Cleveland; and I just have to tell you that we've done so many funerals all our life and had all kinds of religious people—Greek Orthodox, Russian Orthodox, Roman Catholic—of all kinds—Irish, Polish, Slavic, Italian. We've had all kinds of Protestant churches coming in—Fundamentalists, Liberals, whatever you want to call them. We've had humanists give speeches. We've had Rabbis, at various kinds of Jewish synagogues. And I want to tell you, no one ever preaches at a funeral what you've been preaching.

Well, I thought the guy was looking for business, to tell the truth, and I thought that was the line that he told all the new, young, twenty-five year-old clergypersons who came to town. But I thought he still sounded strange because he didn't have to worry about the business in our church. He had it wrapped up. So I just let it go. "Oh, that's interesting." And then he did it again. Then the other funeral director said the same. But, between them they had ninety-nine percent of the church's business.

A long time later, after I had been there a year or two, he finally said it again. I said, "Okay, Steve, what's the story? What have I been saying that you claim you've never heard before?" He said, "You always begin the funeral sermon in any case with the affirmation that God did not create people to die. That God does not will death." And it seems to me that that is a basic affirmation of the Scriptures and Christianity, at least as I understand it.

God did not create people to die. He did not create us to corrupt. He did not create us to be separated. He did not create us to live a few days and years upon the face of the earth and then, for one reason or another, simply to corrupt, to pass away, not to speak of killing each other. That, at least as far as Christians are concerned, is the main doctrine of Christianity, and certainly the center of the Orthodox Church: "Christ is risen from the dead, trampling down death by death and upon those in the tombs giving life."

Isn't that the center of our faith? And isn't it the teaching of the Gospel that God sent His only begotten Son into the world to die so that through His death those who die would be raised to eternal life? Therefore, God does not want death. Death in the Scriptures is an alien. It's called the "last enemy" by the Apostle Paul, to be destroyed and to be overcome by the power of God. Isn't that the teaching? Isn't the whole meaning of the Adam and Eve story, that death came into the world because people refused to lift their hearts and give thanks to God, to accept their creaturehood and tried to be God without God." That the original sin, as Saint Athanasios said, was a reduction of man to himself, and man by himself is "nothing," "corruption."

Therefore, is it not recommended in pastoral counseling, as you walk into a room, to quote the wisdom of Solomon, where it says very particularly, "God did not make death." Death had come into the world by the jealousy of the devil, by the willing rebellion of humanity against God, therefore against his own nature—because our nature is made in the image and according to the likeness of God. And God is life. God is the living God. God does not die. Therefore, if God is life, we are created to live, and that life is connected to truth and to love, primarily. The more that we become God-like, the more we become ourselves and the more we come alive.

At this point I want to make a confession. I felt it essential to do so since it is our teaching in theology that we'll answer at the last judgment for every secret thought in our hearts. But I have to tell you that there are some words that I don't like. If it were up to me I would never use the word "relationship" again. People are so hung up on relationships that they don't care about other people and things. "My relationship with" and not "God"; my "relationship with my wife." and not "my wife." Another word that I don't like is the term "coping." I felt I had to say that since it was a fact. We're created to *live* not to cope, not to cope with life.

We're created to live because God is alive, and we're created to live forever. And the teaching is, I believe, that this is the law of the Prophets—that the reign of God will come when the dead are raised. Death is the great sin in human life. It is not natural to die. That is why we are offended at death. That's why we weep over death. And as Rabbi Grollman said, "Jesus wept." He knew that He was going to raise Lazarus from the dead. He knew that one minute He would say, "Lazarus, come forth, stinking." When I was a kid always waited for that part in church services. Our Dean used to say, "He's stinking."

It's the shortest verse in the Bible—"Jesus wept." He wept because his friend was not made to corrupt in the tomb. Now it is certainly the teaching of Eastern Orthodox Christianity that God is not stupid. And that He knew when He created us that we would try to transform His glorious creation into a worldly planet of people's bones.

In other words, God knows from all eternity that we die. And we can even say that from all eternity death is built into the *economia*, the plan of God for us. But we got the first affirmation that God does not want death. He does not will death. He does not create us to die. Only then can we say the fact that we die, the fact that we have to deal with death is within the will of God. Then we can say that how we die, when we die, where we die, is still in the hands of God. Jesus said, "No bee will fall from the tree, no bird from the air without God being directly involved." So on that level you can say, when a person dies, it's the will of God.

I went to a funeral once where nearly a whole family was wiped out—the wife and three children—young children. And that's exactly what the priest said at the funeral sermon—"God chose his finest flowers." The priest, in my opinion, should have at least said, "God does not will this tragedy. God does not love death. God had created us for life. If it has happened, we believe in God. We trust God. We don't believe that things just happen. So we have to find the meaning of this tragedy. And we have to plumb the depth of this tragedy. But at the same time, we can say God does not want it. And I hope and I think it is Jesus Christ that died on the cross to raise up these people who have died. And that they will live forever with God because God has loved us so much that He is with us where we are.

That statement of the Rabbi was terrific. I could use it forever and ever. "The highest theology is to be there." The highest theology that we have about God is that He is there, but where are we? That's the main question that God said to Adam after sin. The first words to come out of the mouth of God in the Bible are, "Adam, where are you?" And Adam's answer has to be, "I'm dead, Lord." By the way, according to the story, let's make it clear, God didn't say to Adam, "Eat the fruit of the tree and I'll kill you." He said, "Eat of the fruit of the tree and you will die." There's a big difference.

Now, where is God? Luckily, I can quote the sermon of Saint John Chrysostom. He said. "People often shout out, "Where is God?" Particularly in moments of grief, of sorrow, of pain and injustice." Out of the Auschwitz's and the Gulag's of this world and out of the cancer wards, not to speak of the suburban living room when everybody is still not alive but still existing—Where is God? Is there a difference between being alive and existing? According to the Bible some people are physically dead yet they're alive and some people are existing on this earth but they're dead. But this question, "Where is God?" Chrysostom answered and said, "He's hanging on the cross. That's where He is."

Now, in my theological opinion, and I'll make a testimony here, a God who is not hanging on the cross is not God. In fact, it's easier to justify the world without God, than to justify a world with a God sitting on a cloud, watching us with this crazy thing that we call human existence. But the main theological point, the very essence of the theological point, at least with the theology of the Tradition to which I belong, is that God became man in the person of Jesus. Let's go with St. Paul, who said that although He was in the image of God, He did not cling to His divinity. But He was found on earth in *homeosis tou anthropou*, the form of man. But Paul goes on, not only man, but slave; not only slave, but dead; not only dead, but dead on a cross.

It's written in the Scriptures, "Cursed is everyone who hangs upon the cross. You became a sin for us, who is no sin, You became cursed for us who is the holy one. You became dead for us who is life itself." And the very center of the Christian mystery is that life dies like God dies. Life dies in order to trample down death by death, and to give life to those who are in the tombs. Now with this approach I will just mention the other story.

One time, a young woman, eighteen-years-old, was killed in a tractor trailer accident in Pennsylvania. And, at her funeral, the preacher said, "Brothers and sisters, this woman, young girl, has died. We believe that God has created us for life not death. We believe that Christ is risen from the dead. We believe that no dead will remain in the tomb. We believe that our inability to keep ourselves alive, as the psalm says: "Man cannot keep himself alive," has been solved by God. And so we come with faith, with hope, that this life is not ended but we will live forever. However, the fact that this woman, at such a young age, was cut down; the fact that she was senselessly, ridiculously killed and the fact that we still believe, un-like some others, that according to the Scriptures, God kills and God makes alive, and all of it's in the providence of God; then let us pledge before the icons and the altar that we will not let God go until He tells us why this particular death has to take place in this way."

Job, who was mentioned, already said, "Naked I came to the world. Naked I go to the Lord. The Lord gives, the Lord takes away." That's Chapter One. There's fifty more chapters to that book. And he said, "Even though you kill me, you are God. Now tell me—why?" As the Rabbi mentioned, Jesus Himself screamed from the cross with a loud voice, quoting Psalm Twenty-Two, "My God, my God, Why?" It's no sin to ask God, "Why?" Especially if Jesus Christ claims that God is our Father and we are not slaves but children. And He calls us friends. The Master lets you know but the slave doesn't know what the Master is doing—the child does.

Now I have to assume that I remember many people were scan-dalized. Isn't this the will of God? Isn't it just a mystery? Aren't you supposed to be quiet? Aren't you supposed to repress it? Again, anyway, you have all this other kind of, to quote the Rabbi, "gar-bage" coming out like, "Well, God took her because it's better in Heaven." Did you ever notice how much better it is here before peo-ple die and how much better it is in Heaven after?

People, I think, are totally crazy. I would just advise people not to go around when someone is sick and dying and use every possi-ble means—usually calling the priest after all professional help fails, if they're not superstitious about the fact that this priest showing up means instant death. But at the same time, after a person dies, they end up just hanging around funeral homes. And hear what peo-ple say. They'll say, "Well, they're going to a better place." "Well, it's awful here anyway." "Well, you gotta die sometime." So, it's all a totally platonistic view that the soul goes to some kind of bet-ter Heaven. I got news for you. The immortality of the soul detached, going to "a better Heaven," where it contemplates purely spiritual realities, had nothing to do with the Bible.

Earlier this morning the doctor mentioned the Hemlock Society. Socrates drank hemlock. And there's a very interesting theological book written by a Swiss Protestant named Oscar Coolman called *Immortality or Resurrection*, where he compares Jesus' dying and Socrates' dying. We hope Socrates' death is a liberation. How many times have you heard that from Christians? I thought death was the first enemy to be destroyed. "You go to a better place." So what did Socrates do? He says, "Good-bye is a prison. Now the spirit will fly off with the angels."

Sometimes even people have taught children that babies who die become angels. One time in Jamaica, New York I spoke with children at church school. Every Wednesday afternoon I used to have the kids and I asked them, "What's an angel?" And they said, "It's a dead baby." It's totally incredible what's being said.

A lot of people look at Jesus and wonder. Not only did he weep before raising Lazarus, but before His own death He thanked God, sweating blood: "Lord, if it is possible, Father, let this cup pass. But not my will, but Thy will be done." And then He said his heart was heavy. His spirit was groaning. He didn't want to die. He knew what death is. Death is, to quote an ancient saying, "the wages of sin is death." But he knows what death's origin is. Death is the opposite of communion, relationships, expression and so on. In fact, in the Bible, the Psalms, the worst thing about being dead is that you're passing out of "union with God." Who can praise you in shade? In the pit? It's terrible.

I like all these quotes. I told my wife, "If I die first and she doesn't tell whoever is chanting to sing the entire *Troparia* at my funeral, she's going to get it when we meet again. Because that *Troparia* is fantastic. It's a dialogue—and the refrain of the dialogue is, "Halleluhah." And it goes something like this. The priests all gather around the body. And they start singing. They say, "Brothers let us weep and lament for our brother who is with us dead." And, by the way, weeping and lamentation is absolutely theologically in order.

That's why whatever happens when you die, you're with the Lord. You don't go to Heaven on a cloud. You are somehow with the Lord. And, hopefully, that "with the Lord" is something that will come and come quickly for all of us. We pray that way. "Thy Kingdom come." "Come, Lord. Come, quickly." That's what we're hoping for. Our hope is there.

But anyway, even when Steven is killed, it says in the Book of Acts, "And they buried him with great lamentation." Because death even for a Christian is tragic. It's a tragedy. It's a victory of the devil. Economically, a lot of it is even used by God but it is ultimately to be destroyed—not to be glorified and not to be praised. And certainly not to be naturally accepted.

Now, in the funeral service, it says, "Come let us sit. Let us look
at our brother who is dead. And he is dead. And he cannot be dead.
Sing, 'Hallelujah.' " The whole church sings—at least in the Russian Church they sing: "Hallelujah"—the whole crowd. Then
another priest reads a line and says, "But from the mouth of the
dead, death is speaking." He said, "Yes, I am dead, brother. It's
terrible to be dead, you know. So please sing for me." "Hallelujah," the Lord said, "Hallelujah." Then the other priest comes back
and says, "Yes, but we know that Christ had entered death and that
He has died and killed death of Himself. Lord, so let's sing to Him,
'Hallelujah. Hallelujah.' " And it keeps going on like that. And then,
finally, he gets to two words. Finally, they say, "Listen, we've been
talking too much. Let's just all sing to our Lord, 'Hallelujah.' "
And that "Hallelujah" is in Psalm Nineteen. It is the psalm of
victory.

Now we believe that this death has been trampled down. That
the death has been overcome by God Himself in human flesh who
dies upon the tree of the cross becoming what we are that we can
become what He is. We are dead. He is life. He dies so we can live.
That's the center of Christian theology. Now what that means, then,
is that when we relate to death, we must relate to it as an enemy
to be conquered by our faith—to be conquered: to be conquered
by our hope. Ultimately to be conquered by our love—by that God
who is love. That's why we preach, "Christ curcified. Christ risen,"
In fact, the early Christians were preaching the resurrection very
much. I like that place in Acts where they come to Athens; Paul
is preaching to the people. And it says, they come there and they
say that they're teaching about a new God, speaking of foreign dei-
ties. They thought this was a new goddess, in the Pantheon. Wasn't
Jesus dead? No—because the resurrection was preached! In the act
of the Apostles, the only thing we have to preach is Christ risen—
the Messiah glorified—death destroyed, bearing witness to that fact
until He comes again on the clouds to bring this Kingdom of Life
and God and to raise the dead. Now this approach to death means
we don't glorify it. We don't naturalize it. And I will even dare say
that theologically the ultimate approach to death—you know how
in all this literature now they have these stages to death: denial,
bargaining, and then, the last one is acceptance—acceptance of the
reality of death. Now I would say from our theological perspective
of our tradition, that that's great. That's fine. We must accept
death. We must accept the fact that we die. And we must put it at

the center of our life, life and death. That's the only issue, really. The rest are details. In fact, that's the only issue of all the great religions of the world.

I teach at a Buddhist school in the summertime. And they asked the Zen master, "What do you meditate for all those eight straight hours all day? And he said, "Life and death." And, of course, all this covering over of death, denying death, not mentioning death— that's what causes all the trouble when someone finally dies. So, facing death, accepting the fact of death, accepting my dying, the dying of others, that's theologically correct in the Christian tradition. In fact, in the claim of the spiritual values of our tradition is that every person every day should remember that they are going to die. And then don't worry. As the seminarian once translated fro Russian, "Remember to die." It's not "remember to die," it's remember that you're going to die." Remember death.

And sometimes, even our tradition was considered to be very morbid with our funeral practice, bringing the dead person in, putting them on the kitchen table. All the people coming in and weeping. People have been reminiscing about their childhood. I used to make money as a kid. On the northside of Endicott, New York, reading the Psalter over dead bodies in people's living rooms. They had a tradition that one Psalter had to be read when somebody died and I used to go there and people would be walking around— drinking, smoking, talking about the guy. And I'd be sitting there next to the body—on the little chair after the priest finishes, reading. "Rise ye Christians, rise above."

But the whole point is we can still do all that, usually making the cross more beautiful, more pieces of glass on it than ever. And asking why it's three bars in our cross just to change the subject, so that we won't see that the center of our fate is a crucified, loving God, and at the center of our spiritual life is a crucified life. "We're baptized to die and to be risen already. And the Christian spirituality is of those who are already dead before they die and are raised before they're risen. Because we are to live as people belonging to the Kingdom. And at the center of that light, "If you will be my disciple, we will take up the cross." That light is suffering. Life is the victory over death. It's got to be at the center of it. Not morbidly but just realistically.

So that fact of accepting death is essential. You see it even in our classical Christian tradition. I love that line in the story of Flannery O'Connor. She's a Southern writer. Terrific! Highly recommended.

In this story, everyone dies, usually, but she wasn't afraid of death at all. She died herself at the age of thirty-eight from lupus. While she was dying, she wrote this story. In one of the stories these old country folk in the South are talking about strange behavior in these foreigners, the Roman Catholics whom they hated. She was Roman Catholic. And so in one of the stories she has one of the characters say, "And you know, them monks used to actually put their coffins in their rooms, and sometimes at night, they would even sleep in them." And then the other character says, "Yep. They weren't as advanced as we is." You know, as if advancement means you no longer face the fact of death.

In New York they had an incredible newscaster named Ernie Anastos, who's Greek Orthodox. It's very interseting. He's a handsome Greek God on the eleven o'clock news with this brilliant Pepsodent smile. I mean he is just bubbling effervescently with life itself. You know, and it's millions of dollars getting the news on the radio most of which is tragic, especially in New York. I heard him speak once. "How is it that you can do that job and have such a personality and keep going?" You know what he answered? He said, "Because my Yiayia took me to Boston when I was little and she said to me, "Ernie, you see all this stuff. It's all going to be here when we're gone. And we're going to die. And so what you do with your life is very important. Because you're going to die!" And he says, "To tell the truth, one of the secrets of my life for success is every day I get up in the morning and after I say a proper good morning I say, "Ernie, you're going to die."

Now it's acceptance of the death. I would say, theologically at least, in our tradition, acceptance of death is not the final word. The final word, or at least for the Christian Orthodox Church, is the destruction of death by our own death in the imitation of Jesus Christ—namely the transfiguration of death into an act of life. And that is, I would submit to you, what we claim to be—that, God, in Christ and the spirit of the Church.

Our communion is a communion with a body *broken* and blood *shed*, and the conflict of our life and our preaching Christ and Him crucified. The real Christian triumph and victory is when we can transform death into an act of life. And I would submit that that is what we must preach to ourselves and to others. This is what we have to do. Because Christ has come and is crucified and is raised. That act is the ultimate enemy, the total opposite of God, the total disintegration, destruction, corruption and the cause of every evil and the unavoidable victory of every evil that we can possibly think of. That very act, miracle of miracles, can be transformed not into an act of separation, dissolution, corruption and victim of the devil and death, that it can become, itself, an act of a victory.

I would claim that faith is the power of transforming death into an act of life. It's the power of transforming the ultimate separation into the act of ultimate communion. It's the trick, like the Church fathers like to say, of taking the greatest victory of the devil and transforming it into a victory. And we know about them, as John Chrysostom says in the pastoral homily that we read in all of our churches on Easter night, "Christ has risen and life is. Life reigns."

One more point here. Now it seems to me, that the moment of truth about life itself is the moment of death. How we deal with death and how we deal with our own death is the ultimate witness, of our entire life. And it's very interesting and I can't resist to just put it into these concrete terms how one approaches that.

This morning when the doctor was speaking about the Hemlock Society and what goes through your mind when you think of cancer, when you think of death and so on, two things immediately came to my mind. He said that what many people fear most when they fear death is that that's the end of it. That's the end of their useful business. They don't want to be burdens to anybody else.

I love that story of the Russian "Letters of Direction," where an old woman wrote to the monk Maharlay. She said, "I wish that I could just die because I'm very sick and I'm going to be a burden on my children. What should I do?" And the monk says, "Who the hell do you think you are? Maybe God wants you to be a burden on your child. Maybe it's your child's salvation. Humble yourself for God's sake and be a burden." There's also the story of the president of the Union Theological Seminary in New York who, when he could no longer speak because he had cancer in his larynx, killed himself. A professor of Systematic Theology, saying, "I'm now of no use anymore." That theology is not the one that I would subscribe to, because still God is the Lord. And maybe, just maybe, how that man would handle the cancer and what he would do with it may have been more important than every sermon he ever gave, every class he ever taught, every book he ever wrote.

Which leads to the second point, what to do when you have

cancer. When the doctor said to our theological dean, "What does it mean when you hear that word cancer?" I would dare to say that when Father Schmemann heard the word cancer, all of the usual things went through his mind. And there was certainly one thing more, and that was what he shared with our community, "Brothers and sisters, the hour has come. It is time to show what we really, really know. It's an opportunity of witness like no other opportunity. It's an opportunity of glorifying God."

You know it's very interesting. One of the nuns of Saint Theresa Babina came to her one day and said, "Mother, what should we do to glorify God and to prove our unswerving resolve and our lingering faith?" And Saint Theresa said to this novice nun, "What are you asking me for? Ask His Glorious Son." The way God is glorified according to the Scripture is in His crucifixion. That's how we begin the Holy Thursday twelve readings. "Now the Son of Man is glorified. And God is glorifying again. And when I am lifted up off the earth, I will draw all things to myself." Now we are supposed to imitate that. That is what we're supposed to do if we are indeed baptized, anointed, sealed, chrismated children of God in Jesus Christ.

So we can really say that a real believer was just waiting for that death to come, in order to take it on and to destroy it. And I can actually say that Schmemann had said as much, in the chapel shortly after the doctor's news. He said, "All my life I've been teaching about the Eucharist, that broken body, that spilled blood. All my life I've been knocking establishments and all this kind of thing." "And knowing a little bit now about God," he said, "people have said to me, 'Why did God do this to Father Alexander?' " And he said, "In a sense, God didn't have any choice. A person who talked as much as I did had to able to show something. In a sense it's very much like a God."

I love what he said—"But pray to God that you all get what you need around here," he said. "But most of all, pray that whatever God wants from this, it would be done—and for me and I now have the opportunity to at least somehow be a witness in my life to what I have been preaching, teaching all my life."

So death is, for a Christian, the opportunity par excellance to suffer meaningfully. I loved it when the Rabbi said, "You know, you're not going to remove suffering, but you should remove the stupid suffering, the misplaced suffering, the neurotic suffering." Not every suffering is the cross of Christ in the dogma of the soul.

Some suffering is just because we're sinful, stupid and dumb. And that doesn't redeem anything. But when Saint Paul can bear to write to the Colossians, "We fullfill what is lacking in the suffering of Christ for the sake of His Body, the Church," there's a theological truth there. The Lord Christ is not Jesus by Himself. The Lord Christ is Jesus of all the suffering, victimized poor of the earth. That's what He told us Christians. And we who will believe in Him consciously put ourselves into His body. We dare even to call ourselves the Body of Christ. And we bear what Saint Paul said to the Corinthians: "in our bodies the dying of Jesus so that we can live with Him." And, therefore, the approach of Christians to death is not only to remember death, to accept the fact of death, not to cover it over, not to whitewash it, not to naturalize it, not to make it in any way anything good, but leaving it rotten!

All the stuff that we said to the doctor in the beginning—rotten, sorrowful, grieving, yucky, blah! You know, everything comes out to the surface at that moment. You see what it is and then to take it and to save it. Because Christ is crucified and Christ is raised. And His Spirit is given to me. I will take all that rotten on myself and in myself and I can transform it by the power of the Spirit into what we say about Jesus—and what they all told us of His death in our Liturgy.

And the life created death and that death then becomes an act of life. And whenever anyone has participated in the death of a real Christian and certainly on the pastoral night in the church of the clergy, we know that though death is still a tragedy, that it goes to believe and obey God—that it is not tragedy but a victory!

Chapter Six

THE UNITY OF BODY, MIND AND SOUL:
A MEDICAL PERSPECTIVE

Herbert Benson

Well over a half of us will die in the United States of heart attacks and strokes. Now it is not so disturbing that we are going to
die of that disease because, after all, we have ot die of something!
But what is problematic is that more and more young people are
being afflicted with this disease at younger and younger ages. As
a cardiologist, I became interested in this—and tried, with many
others, to understand what the underlying disease process is so we
can do something about it.

The fact that more and more people are dying of this disease was
pointed out by several physicians in the 1960s and 1970s in several
studies. For example, the late Dr. Samuel Levine, who practiced at
the Peter Bent Brigham Hospital noted that the sons of fathers he
was treating were developing their heart disease at an average age
that was 13 or 14 years younger than their fathers had developed
theirs. In other words, the sons were developing heart disease much
younger than their fathers had. And then we noticed in the hospitals
that for the first time, men and women in their 40's and 30's and
indeed sometimes in their 20's were coming in with heart attacks and
strokes. This was so frequent and so common that the young interns and residents starting off their careers thought this to be a matter of course while just five to ten years prior to that to see a heart
attack or stroke in a young person would be so rare as to lead to
its description in the medical literature.

By far the most common underlying feature in heart attack or
stroke is something called atherosclerosis—or hardening of the arteries. What happens in this process is an artery or aorta, in particular,

becomes clogged or blocked; and an artery is the major distributing conduit for the blood. Arteries go to various organs and are carried there from the heart. So is an artery is blocked, the essential nutrients—oxygen and foodstuffs—cannot be carried to the organ and the tissues of that organ may die. If this happens in the brain, we are talking about a stroke. If this blockage occurs in one of the heart vessels, the coronary vessels, where what is downstream from the blockage is heart muscle tissue, the tissue may die. This is a "heart attack"—or a coronary or a myocardial infarction, all meaning the same thing. Should this occur in the kidney, the kidney may become shrunken and diseased.

Alright then, what causes atherosclerosis? There are several major incriminating features. One of them is diet. We have heard a great deal about the amount of cholesterol we eat and the amount of fats in our diet, because these fats are part of the material that ultimately leads to the blockage within the artery. Indeed, we have changed a good part of our national diet because of that. Now we do not eat quite so many fats, specifically, saturated fats; there are many substitutes.

We have been asked to cut down on eggs, butter and other rich foods. The answer cannot, however, be found in diet alone. There are still arguments as to the overall importance, the risk versus benefit, of diet in this process. But there is no question whatsoever that blood pressure is related to atherosclerosis. The higher one's blood pressure, the more rapidly atherosclerosis will develop. The lower one's blood pressure, the more protected one is. Alright, what causes high blood presure? Here again there are some major problems because over 95% of cases of high blood pressure are due to unknown causes. And for lack of better terms, we call this "essential hypertension"; "hypertension" not meaning being hypertense, but meaning high blood pressure—and "essential" meaning unknown. There are between 23 and perhaps 50 to 60 million adult Americans who suffer from high blood pressure. This is no surprise because when we look at the death rate, we should expect this many people to have high blood pressure; yet, in over 95% of the cases, we do not know the cause of the disease.

A number of years ago, several of us felt that psychological disturbances, that being unable to cope with situations, in short, that stress and its related behavioral adjustments might play an important role in the development of high blood pressure. In fact, this notion has even crept into our speech: "Keep your cool, keep your blood pressure down." But it is extremely difficult to quantify stress; while we can measure blood pressure quite accurately, what would be stressful for one person might not be stressful for another.

More recently, evidence has evolved from a number of different sources; first, from studies of population, epidemiologic studies, where it was shown that under certain circumstances certain people living in the cities tended to have high blood pressure. For example, people living in the cities tended to have higher blood pressure than people living in the country. Take the people from their rural areas, move them into the urban areas, and their blood pressure would increase. At certain times of the year certain groups of people tended to have higher blood pressure. Who for example do you think in this country would have the highest blood pressures as a group around March or April? Accountants and CPA's. When would students have their highest blood pressure? Exam time. Athletes? Before the game. Soldiers? During war, going into battle.

In the Second World War, when the German troops had the city of Leningrad surrounded, people in that city had higher blood pressures when the Germans were there as opposed to after the Germans left. I've often wondered who had the inclination and the time under those circumstances to measure blood pressure, but it was done with a rigid approach. You might remember Texas City, Texas, after the Second World War, in 1948. There were two ships containing ammonia nitrate photosynthesizer which blew up with the force equivalent to several of the bombs dropped on Hiroshima. Windows were damaged within a fifty-mile radius with the blast being heard within that range. People within earshot of this developed high blood pressure which lasted about six months and then gradually returned to normal.

More recently, on Three Mile Island, the people living there tended to develop high blood pressure with the threat of nuclear radiation exposure. This kind of thing can be observed in animals as well as people. If you take mice and rats and overcrowd them, they will have higher blood pressure than their own systems can control. Take a mouse, place it in a cage with a hungry cat walking around the cage and that mouse will develop high blood pressure. The Russians did one experiment some of us found disturbing; they put families of baboons, characteristically made up of one male and his harem of females, into a cage. They allowed such a family to become established. They they removed the original male from the cage, put him in a nearby cage where he could watch, and replaced him with a new male. Under these somewhat stressful circumstances the original male now watching developed high blood pressure within six weeks and the poor animal died of either a heart attack or a stroke within a year.

We think we understand the mechanism in which such stressful events are translated into high blood pressure. All mammals possess within themselves a response called the emergency response, or the fight or flight response. This resides within an area of the brain called the hypothalamus. And in an area within the hypothalamus, one stimulus leads to a coordinated secretion within the body of adrenaline, and more adrenaline; epinephrine, and more epinephrine; which then leads to a whole host of coordinated changes—increased heart rate, increased blood pressure, sweating, a three to four hundred percent increase in the amount of blood flow through our muscles, and an increase in our metabolism—a very important preparedness.

About 60 years ago, Dr. Walter B. Cannon of the Harvard Medical School reasoned that this preparedness was for running or for fighting. Thus the name, the fight or flight response. Under stressful circumstances, we elicit this response. This was most eloquently shown by the Czech physiologist, Dr. Jan Borg. What he did was take healthy medical students, have them lie quietly, and hooked them up to instruments that would measure heart rate, blood pressure, skeletal muscle blood flow and bodily metabolism. Then he told them, "Alright, I want you to do a very simple thing: I'm going to give you a four digit number like 6246. From that I want you to subtract 17. You're going to get an answer. And from that, subtract 17. And you do that as quickly as possible. The students were also told not to be bothered by a metronome clicking in the background. Click, click, click. Why should you be bothered by your fellow medical students who will give you encouragement? Encouragement that took a form you can well imagine. "You know I can do better than that—come on let's go." Within two seconds of having to start the subtraction, within two seconds of the stimulus, they exhibited the increased heart rate, increased blood pressure, sweating, increased rate of breathing and marked increase in the amount of blood flow through their muscles.

This is the type of situation most of us face daily working under pressure to perform certain tasks. And what has been shown repeatedly is that the elicitation of this response is translated from transient to more or less permanent elevations in blood pressure. Hence the secenario of apparently stressful events, acting through the fight

or fight response leading to high blood pressure, later to atherosclerosis and perhaps ultimately to some of the major causes of death
we face in the Western world today.

We live in an extremely stressful world under what I believe are
the most stressful circumstances man has ever lived. Not that in the
past Man did not face death, pestilence and uncertainties, but there
was a certain predictability about life. Yes, there were Huns on the
horizon or what have you, and one could not predict when a famine
would occur, but one lived with and accepted these facts as part of
life. In our existence today, we are promised too much; we are almost promised that it is alright to live forever, that it is almost un-
American to develop a disease.

Our expectations are too high—but evern worse is the unpredic-
tability we have to live with. We do not know from whence stimuli
will come, nor do we have standards by which to react to them appropriately. The near assassination of a president, the near assassination of a Pope, rampant violence, the gruesome material in our
nightly local news, where the credo of some of the local stations is,
"If it bleeds, it leads," where uncertainties come repeatedly . . . take,
for example, this Tylenol business. How do you respond to it? You
are taking pills. You feel you need the pills and suddenly it is a risk
to be taking them. We respond to these events as we are programmed
to respond—with elicitation of the fight or flight response. And ultimately this does us harm, because the response that was useful,
naturally choosing either to run or to fight effectively, no longer
serves us because in these situations it is no longer acceptable to run
or fight. For example, if you were upset with Tylenol, what would
you do about it? Would you hit the person next to you, or start running about the room? Such responses are socially inappropriate, yet
our bodies act in such a fashion. Such behavior will breed anxiety
and disquiet, inability to get along with others, and a host of symptoms that go along with such disquiet including nausea, vomiting,
diarrhea, constipation, inability to communicate with others, and
the inability to sleep well. These symptoms lead to worsening underlying diseases; if we suffer from something like arthritis, or back
pain, or headache, these problems are made worse by stress. What
can we do about it?

Fortunately we have within ourselves an opposite response, which
is the physiologic opposite to the fight or flight response, and it is
this we call the relaxation response. It was first described by a Nobel
prize winning Swiss physiologist, Dr. Walter Hess; it was he who

found the part of the brain that when stimulated brought forth the fight or flight response that Dr. Cannon described earlier. He found another area within the hypothalamus that when stimulated brought about physiologic changes that were the counterpart, the exact opposite to the fight or flight response. He called this, and I quote, "a protective mechanism against the harmful effects of overstress."

We came upon this in humans about fifteen or so years ago when I was studying in the laboratory of Dr. Barger at the Harvard Medical School. We were working on a model for behaviorally induced high blood pressure through the use of stress. We were able successfully to show that stress could lead to high blood pressure in monkeys. And while these experiments were going on, some young people came to the laboratory and said, essentially, "Why are you fooling around with monkeys? Why don't you study us; we feel we can effectively control our blood pressure. We practice transcendental meditation."

This was 1968, this was the Harvard Medical School; we were having enough trouble convincing people stress could be related to high blood pressure. I told the young people to go away. I really did not want a thing to do with them. Fortunately, they would not leave; they hung around day after day, and insisted that they be studied. Reasoning little would be lost in having a look at whether or not meditation might lead to some physiological changes, we decided to begin our studies of these individuals. And what I shall describe now are some of the physiological changes that occur in this state, but please keep in mind that there is nothing unique about transcendental meditation. As you will see, this state can be achieved in many, many different fashions. But from a historical point of view transcendental meditation was the first description of this state in humans, so let me describe it for you.

About the time we started our experiments Drs. Robert P. Wallis and Archie Wilson started theirs at the University of California. Wallis joined me at Harvard; by pure chance our experimental designs were exactly the same and we were able to collate our data and describe the physiologic changes. The experiments consisted of people coming to the laboratory, having instruments placed on them, intra-arterial needles, catheters and tubes placed in arteries and veins. These instruments measured and collected the amount of gas being expired. Electrodes were placed on their bodies to measure various electrical phenomena, their brain waves being measured by an electroencephelograph. We had the people sit quietly for an entire hour, getting used to the instruments. To begin, for twenty minutes we obtained baseline measurements, the resting measurement. They were then asked to start meditating. They did nothing other than change what they were thinking about; there was no change in their activities, no change in their posture. All they did was start following some meditative instructions. We made other measurements.

Then we asked them to stop meditating and to go back to their regular everyday thoughts. We found rather profound changes. The hallmark of the state is a decrease in the metabolism of the body. There was a 16 to 17 percent decrease from resting, in the amount of oxygen being consumed, that is the amount of fuel being burned by the body. And all that was changed was what the subjects thought about. These changes lasted as long as the subjects followed the meditative instruction. When asked to stop, they returned to baseline or to normal. This was paralleled by decreases in the amount of carbon dioxide being produced, which means that another measure, called respiratory quotient did not change; these people were not hyperventilating (for example, by breathing quickly and holding their breath).

This was a true decrease in the amount of fuel being burned by the body. Also significant was a decrease in the amount of air being moved. In our experiments the subjects' breathing decreased from approximately 13 to 11 breaths per minute. Subsequently, our group as well as others have had the opportunity to measure advanced meditation—to observe yogis and Tibetan Buddhist monks, whose rate of breathing was down to zero to one breath per minute. Essentially, these individuals stopped breathing for three to four minutes, and then returned to normal without breathing rapidly. There was marked lowering in the amount of fuel being required by the body. And interestingly, the amount of oxygen being carried in the blood to the cells, the amount of "food" to the cells was normal. The cells were getting enough oxygen, they were just using less. Well, we wondered, perhaps were we looking at a state of hibernation. Perhaps man was able to hibernate in a fashion that was previously thought impossible. Another way to look at hibernation, other than looking at the decreased metabolism, is to look at temperature. A hibernating animal will decrease his rectal temperature two to three tenths of a degree. How many of you think bears hibernate? May I have a show of hands? Most of you do. Bears do not hibernate. My reason for asking this is my admiration for two brother physiologists who could determine if bears were sleeping or hibernating in mid-winter. Armed only with rectal thermometers they entered caves where bears were mostly asleep or hibernating, and made their measurements. Indeed, they found out that the bears were sleeping and not hibernating. Continuing their measurements until they woke one of their subjects, who was upset and chased them from the cave, they escaped unharmed and feeling their debt to science had been paid, recorded their results in medical literature. I am fond of that story; I tell it whenever I can.

Under much less hazardous circumstances, we were able to measure rectal temperature in people practicing meditation and found there was no decrease in rectal temperature; therefore, at least in man, this is not a hibernatory state. There were brain wave changes, however; the changes showed a marked slowing and a production of Alpha waves and Theta waves—very slow waves that have been associated with feelings of peace and tranquility. It is important to recognize that these physiologic changes are distinctly different from those which occur during sleep. For example, in the oxygen consumption decreases that occur within three to five minutes of meditation occur to a lesser degree over four to five hours of sleep, followed by a gradual return to normal.

Brain wave changes are different, as are other bodily metabolic changes. But it did look as if we were having a human counterpart to our tests—namely, an opposite response to the inborn fight or flight response. If that were the case, it made no sense at all that transcendental meditation would be the only way to bring this about. It would be as if to say there was only one way to perspire, or one way to increase one's heart rate, which is silly.

So all we did at that point was look at the four basic steps of transcendental meditation: the first was sit quietly in a comfortable position, the second was close your eyes, the third was have a repetitive word, sound or prayer in your consciousness, and fourth was passively disregard any other thoughts which might come to mind and return to the repetition. Using these four steps as guidelines, we looked to the religious and secular literatures of the world to see whether or not these steps had been described in these texts. What we found, following three to four years of study, was that in virtually every single culture of man, the same exact steps were being practiced.

Let me run through them by way of example: the earliest examples we found were the Ypanishads, the Hindu Scriptures, dating back to the seventh century B.C., where it was written, "To achieve a union with God, sit quietly by yourself, pay attention to your breathing and on each outbreath say silently to yourself a word from the Scriptures. Should other thoughts come to mind, passively disregard them and come back to the repetitions." The next example we found was within Judaism, dating back to the time of the second temple, which was from the second century B.C. to the first century A.D. and within a school of thought called McCaballism. People who were in this school would assume a fetal-like posture—a sort of squatting—and rock from heel to toe, on each outbreath repeating over and over the name of the magic seal.

In Christianity, prayers dating back to the time of Christ Himself evolved and were passed on by word of mouth through the monastery, cropping up occasionally and surviving in the Middle Ages; for example, there is a twelfth-century work—"The Cloud of Unknowing"—an anonymous work from England but ultimately being codified on Mount Athos in Greece in the fourteenth century, where as you know there are Greek Byzantine monasteries. The instructions proscribed twice daily, were sit quietly, pay attention to your breathing, and on each outbreath say silently to yourself, "Lord Jesus Christ, have mercy." Should other thoughts come to mind, passively disregard them and come back to the repetition. Of course, you will recognize this has survived into the modern form that is currently called the Jesus Prayer. At the same time, in the fourteenth century in northern Europe, there was the Jewish catalystic, mystic tradition evolving; and the Rabbi Abulafia, working within that school, wrote: "To achieve the state, sit quietly, pay attention to your breathing, and on each outbreath, say silently to yourself the words, the components, that make up God's name (sounds like Adonai)." A similar practice may be found in Islam, where the process is called Bhikr, and a repeated word, a prayer, is called a *wird*.

In Zen Buddhism, people count to ten in magical numbers on each outbreath and then come back to one again over and over, disregarding other thoughts that may come to mind. In Tibetan Buddhism, people carry prayer beads and throughout the day say the prayer *Om Mani Padmep Hum* over and over—Hail, jewel of the lotus. Virtually the same thing happens in Shintosim, Taoism, and Confucionism. Only the words are different. In the more primitive, if you will, chauvinistic religions, the same state would be achieved by chanting in time to the stamping of feet or beating of a gong. Here in New England about a hundred years ago there was a school of thought called Nature and Mysticism.

Thoreau, Emerson and Alcott belonged to that school close by Concord. They would achieve that state by fixed gazing at light as it shimmered off nearby leaves. Thoreau, on his table at Walden Pond set two books: one was the Hindu Scriptures, the *Bhagavid Gita,* and on many occasions compared himself to a yogi. In England, Wordsworth described this beautifully in his poem, "Refection by Tintern Abbey," where he would achieve this state by fixed gazing at light as it shimmered off a nearby waterfall. Alfred Lord Tennyson, who liked himself a great deal—used to walk down the street saying his own name over and over—"Tennyson, Tennyson, Tennyson."

We reasoned that in observing any one of these techiniques we might find the same physiologic changes that we found in transcendental meditation. So what we did was go back to the laboratory, bring in some bright Harvard University, Simmons College and Boston College students and give them instructions adapted directly to Zen Buddhism. They were told to sit quietly, close their eyes, pay attention to their breathing and on each outbreath (one, two, three, up to ten, and back to one), passively disregard everyday thoughts when they came to mind.

The experiment was a complete and inexorable failure. What happened was that the bright students lost count, panicked and that was the end of the experiment. We decided to make things simple for them. We asked them to stay with the number one. When we did that, we found exactly the same changes found in transcendental meditation. Next, we brought in people who prayed regularly; not a beseeching prayer asking for something, but: in Catholicism, a Rosary kind of prayer; in Judaism, a divining kind of prayer. We found the same changes. In other words, the prayer, the *sound* used does not matter. If the steps described above are carried out, these physiologic changes will occur. As I stated at the outset, what I am saying here is in no way a scientific or mechanistic explanation of prayer. Rather, it is a reaffirmation of the religious thought of many centuries, that prayer is good for you. As you may now see, such thought is correct.

Our next step was to see whether the regular elicitation of this response had usefulness in the therapy of diseases related to stress—increased adrenaline, increased noradrenaline, increased epinephrine, increased norepinephrine; and of course high blood pressure. What we found—and this has now been verified by at least several designated laboratories—is that the regular elicitation of the relaxation response, regardless of method, significantly lowers blood pressure.

This lowering occurs not only when you are practicing (for example, when you are praying) but carries over into other periods of the day.

Now, if any of you suffer from high blood pressure, you should be taking pills for this, because the drugs lower blood pressure and decrease the risk of atherosclerosis, therefore decreasing your chances of contracting these other dire diseases. And if you choose to elicit the relaxation response, you should check with your physician first because as you lower your blood pressure your medication might have to be adjusted. Only a physician can appropriately do that. However, if your blood pressure is normal, and you are not taking medications, the side effects of what we are talking about are those of prayer. If prayer is dangerous, this is dangerous.

Prayer has usefulness for patients in many other disease states such as extra heartbeats or arhythmias. One of my fellow physicians, a Greek Orthodox, was given the number one to repeat in prayer over and over again and his extra heartbeat—which in this case was quite serious, something called ventricular tachycardia, actually got worse. Observing this, the physician asked, "What is going on?" The patient replied, "Well, this is like voodoo to me. Is there something more compatible that I might use instead of the number one?" So he was wisely given *Kyrie Eleison* and with that his condition markedly improved. The physician used the patient's belief system, and using this, doctor and patient were able to work together.

I will come back to this idea that the word, prayer or phrase you choose should conform to the belief system of the person whom you are teaching. Extra heartbeats, various kinds of arhythmias, most forms of anxiety—headache, nausea, vomiting, diarrhea, insomnia— the symptoms I mentioned earlier—inability to get along with others, disquiet . . . these can be cured by sitting quietly once or twice daily and listening to your response. About half the people we worked with who had migraines got significantly better, where the headaches were gone and the others had a significant reduction in their headaches.

It is very useful, even in the therapy of more severe kinds of pain, such as the pain of cancer. It does not make the pain go away, but people are better able to live with the pain. The pain is there, but I recognize there is something in me—or given to me, if you will— that is greater than the pain, that allows me to control the pain. And so it is useful in the stess-related disorders that plague our society;

while remaining so remarkably simple. It is a natural thing within us; in fact one of the major problems I have in talking about this is the simplicity. It is this very simplicity that gives us problems because in our day and age we are suspect of something that does not cost. We are suspect of something that is natural. People attach gimmicks like machines to this, but it is there simply for the taking to counteract the harmful effects of stress.

As I alluded to earlier, the word, sound, prayer or phrase should be chosen to conform to your belief system, or to the belief system of the person whom you are teaching. The reason for this is that compliance will be better: if you believe in something, it is something you are going to do. Many of my patients at Beth Israel are Roman Catholic. Rather than giving them the number one, I suggest the Jesus Prayer, "Lord Jesus Christ, have mercy." Indeed, these people welcome this. Too many of them say to me, "Thank you, doctor, thank you for telling me to pray again. It is something I have wanted to do, but felt funny about; but now that you as a doctor tell me that it is good for me, it is something that I will do." That shows the problems we have in our society.

Then, the compliance of Roman Catholic patients with a prayer they believe in is high. With my Greek Orthodox patients we use *Kyrie Eleison*. With my Jewish patients we use something like Shalom, or echaud, meaning one. Protestant patients often choose something from the 23rd Psalm or the Lord's Prayer. For atheistic or agnostic patients, the number one is fine. Others like Eastern techniques, so transcendental meditation is as good as any. What is important is for the patient to believe in what he is repeating. We have worked hand in glove with many religious organizations of all denominations because meditative prayer is physiologically very healthful. In fact, it is healthful in a way we thought previously was possible only through the use of drugs. What the relaxation response does is actually block—we learned with recently with Dr. John W. Hoffman, a young fellow in our laboratory who recently passed away from leukemia—norepinephrine or noradrenaline action in a way that some of the most popular drugs now being used in the Western world today do: the beta-blocker syndrome. You do this naturally.

So we have this capacity with us. Here, you teach methods in your meditative prayer that can bring this about. Bolstered with this physiologic knowledge, I say humbly that perhaps you can use prayer, in addition to its spiritual value, as a valuable tool to promote good health with the regular elicitation of this response.

Chapter Seven

THE UNITY OF BODY, MIND AND SOUL: PASTORAL-PSYCHOLOGICAL PERSECTIVE

Peter Poulos

It's a great joy for me to be back at Hellenic College today and to participate in this symposium on Medicine, Psychology and Religion. The topic for my presentation, "The Unity of Body, Mind and Soul" was not a topic that I chose. It was assigned to me by my good friend, John Chirban. Strangely enough, when I received the brochure with the schedule for the day and saw the topic, I misread it. I read it a number of times for a week as "Body, Mind and Soul". I completely missed "The Unity of." Then one day I picked up the schedule, and suddenly I saw this.

I think the reason I missed "The Unity" is because I work in a setting where I do not see the unity of body, mind and soul—but rather I see the division. I see fragmentation and brokenness. I work in a 550-bed general hospital which is also a teaching hospital with interns and residents. Rather than stay strictly with the topic of "The Unity of Body, Mind and Soul," I would like to describe some of what I see in the hospital—some of the things that relate to body, some of the things that relate to mind, and some of the things that relate to soul. Then, hopefully, at the end, I will bring these things together and discuss how they relate to each other.

I hope to describe some emotional or psychological issues that we see in the hospital and the issues that I would call theological issues, noting how these kind of issues relate to each other. I think that the theology of the Church definitely has something to say to the hospital situation and it is with this that I would want to end my presentation. Let us begin then with a description of what I see

91

a strange experience. When you are first admitted they put a name tag on your wrist—a label that you must wear for identification. This marks your official entrance into that separate world of the patient. As a patient, people will come to you dressed in their white uniforms and begin to do things for you and to you. They will give you directions about what you can and cannot do. You give up a lot of your freedom—you become dependent on other people because you're now a "patient." As a patient you can often feel like a child—a small child. Tests and procedures are done, often with very large equipment that can at first frighten you. You don't really understand what's going on, even if it's been explained. The people around you, the hospital staff, use very technical words—medical jargon—that you don't understand. You're in a foreign territory. It's the medical world! Not understanding all the words adds to the sense of confusion, the anxiety.

The anxiety of being a patient though is also partly due to the uncertainty that has now entered your life. Most of us live our lives believing that we have some control over it. We do have control over some things in our lives. But when illness comes, we recognize that we do not have complete control over our life. When tests are being done and we wait for the results, there's a lot of uncertainty. What are they going to find? How much will it change my life? Will I die? What's happening to me? It can be a frightening experience.

Added to the difficulty is the sense of isolation that patients often feel. You're separated from the family—separated from the people that you work with and from the things you usually do. You can easily feel cut off—cut off from all the things that make you you.One can easily feel that he or she is just a patient—an object—a body—but not a person anymore. I'm not saying that this is always true, but it is often true. We are cut off from the things that make us who we are, from the things that make us the unique persons that we are, from the things that give us some sense of our identity.

I've heard many patients say—"I don't feel like myself anymore. I feel like a stranger to myself." That's isolation! That's being cut-off! We can also feel cut-off from our own body if there is any significant change in our body image. Changes that occur from a stroke, an amputation, a mastectomy, etc., can make us need to get to know our bodies and body image in a new way. I think the situation that I'm describing raises a lot of concern, theologically as well as psychologically.

Theological because one of the relationships that often gets changed or challenged by the situation of being a patient, of being ill, is the relationship with God. On the spiritual level there's often a sense of having been abandoned by God—of being far away from God. Many patients have said, "I can't pray anymore. I pray, but I don't feel like God is here. I can't feel God's nearness." And these are people who could before. In terms of spiritual life, not feeling the presence of God or experiencing Him—feeling abandoned by God—is a great threat, a great challenge. On the level of the mind, God also comes in. Because what gets challenged oftentimes is our theology. I've heard many, many patients struggle with their theology. Some express an awful lot of anger—confusion and anger.

We live our life with certain beliefs. For example, many of us were raised with the belief that if we do the right things, if we try to be good Christians, we will be rewarded and that one of the rewards that God will bless us with will be good health and happiness. Suddenly we become ill, and our theology is challenged. We wonder, what's going on here? I lived up to my part of the bargain—where is God? What do I believe? Where is my theology?

Most of us, I think, live in relationship with God in a way in which we want to control God. We work out some kind of a bargain that helps us to control our life. We believe that God, if we do the right things, will also live up to His part of the bargain. And illness is often the time when this is challenged. Such a theology can crumble. The theological dimension of being ill is that we are faced with our limits. We are faced with the fact that we are human beings—that we're not God. I've often said to my students (and they laugh at me at the beginning when I say it) that my greatest sin for which I will have to answer to God—my greatest sin is that deep down in my gut I want to be God. I want to have that power. I don't want to have limits. That's something with which I struggle.

I said that my students laugh at me when I say this. That is usually at the beginning of the program. By the time they get to the middle or the end of the program, they realize that they have the same difficulty. They see that they too want to be God—or want to be able to control God. They see that they too can become frightened and at times angry with their limitations—the limitations of being human. A big part of what we are dealing with on a daily basis is learning to live with our humanness, learning to live within the limits and trying to become more comfortable with the fact that we are not all powerful—that we are not God.

This connects to the other group of people within the hospital that I want to talk about—this is the staff. Since there are too many staff to talk about, I'll pick one to describe to you briefly: the physician, the doctor. Many physicians struggle with the same thing I've just described: what I would call "wanting to be God." They expect of themselves that they should have all of the answers—all of the knowledge—and they have great difficulty when they cannot perform miracles. When they do the best that they could do, the best that anyone could do, and yet the patient dies—the doctor is confronted with the fact that he or she has limits. In the training of the physicians, I don't believe that they are helped to deal with this.

Just the other night an elderly woman died in Intensive Care and the physician who was on the Code procedure when they tried to resuscitate her was having difficulty because she died. This was a woman in her nineties. He was stalling before calling the family doctor and the nurses were getting angry at him. The chaplain who was on duty that night asked, "Is this your first Code where a patient died?" He said "Yes." He shared that he hadn't thought about what it would be like when this happened. He had never really dealt with it. It's very hard. He and the chaplain talked about this a little, then he went ahead and called the attending doctor. In his head, on an intellectual level, he knew that everything that could have been done for this woman had been done. But on the feeling level, he felt a sense of failure—a sense of having been defeated—and he was struggling with that.

I must tell you I'm glad he was struggling with it because that's a beginning—at least he was able to talk about it and to listen to his own feelings. Many physicians don't. Many physicians have a way of just suppressing their feelings, burying their feelings and of acting as if they are just a "thinking mind." I make that distinction because the mind is also the seat of feelings, not just of thinking. They function completely on a head level. Just as the patient can become only a body and the person is forgotten, we see the same sin being repeated in the doctor. The doctor becomes just an intellectual being, just a "thinking mind." He or she can be so distant from his or her feelings that at times you cannot sense the person at all. What comes across is a coldness, a lack of sensitivity, a professionalism that is without feeling—without care. The whole emphasis is on cure. What doesn't get communicated is the care.

There are ways that physicians, and others in the hospital, can create a lot of distance from their own feelings about what is happening. This tends to add to their becoming solely intellectual beings.

It adds also to the patient becoming an object, just a body. For example, in the hospital, the staff never refer to a patient as having died; the word is "expired." Very often you will hear a physician say to a family, "I'm sorry to tell you this, but the patient expired." The patient—not "your husband," or "your wife" or "your daughter." "The patient expired and I have to ask you a question. We want to have permission to do a post-mortem examination" which means an autopsy. And all of that is feelingless. "The patient expired" doesn't say anything, and "post-mortem examination" doesn't carry with it the "oomph" or feeling that "autopsy" does. So it's all said in a very distant way.

I wondered whether to share with you an incident that happened recently. I don't want you to think, "What kind of hospital is this where he works?" I know though from friends working at other hospitals about the many similar things that occur. The incident I wanted to share occurred just last week, a week ago yesterday. It was a very busy afternoon in the Emergency Room and one of the patients died. The medical resident had to go out and tell the husband that his wife had died. He told the wrong man!

You might ask, "How could that happen?" It happened because it was in the Emergency Room—he didn't know the patient—the person had just been brought in. The doctor didn't take the time to really find out the name. He was directed to the corridor and was told the husband was waiting there. He told the wrong husband. This happened because of the lack of personal touch. If he had only addressed the man by name, or referred to the patient by name, it would have been clear that it was not this man's wife that he was talking about. But that didn't happen. In this case—the patient expired. He didn't take the few minutes to find out who is this person, he simply informed a man that his wife's body had died.

I don't want to sound as if I'm bitter against physicians, because I'm not. I really feel for them. I feel for them because they have an awful lot of responsiblity. I feel for them because they struggle with many of the same things that I struggle with—I see a lot of myself in physicians. I want to reach out to them—help them to be who they are, help them to have their own reactions, their own emotions and to let these come through to people—not to allow themselves to become just the highly professional machine—the highly professional thinking but feelingless mind—that deals with curing bodies.

I mentioned the similarities that I see between myself and

physicians; I would say between the clergy and physicians. Clergy struggle with their own limits, much the way physicians do. Tremendous parallels exist between the two. Both are often very driven—driven to learn, driven to grow, driven to succeed. Both are separated from other people. Both, by the way, clergy and doctors, often make terrible patients. They don't live very well within limits. It raises an awful lot of anxiety because they are used to it. They're used to being in a powerful position.

I mentioned earlier how physicians often will use their knowledge in a way that creates some distance from their feelings. One of the things that I see in some clergy and seminary students is this same pattern. They have all the theological answers. Their theology is so solid, but very often a lot of it is out of their head. It is knowledge about God. "Knowledge about" and "experiencing" are not always the same. They can't experience what the patient is experiencing. They don't enter into the patient's experience—it is foreign to them. They cannot understand what the struggle is. If you have faith, if you have these beliefs, then what are you worried about? What are you anxious about?

This leads to the last part of my presentation which is how theology relates to this human experience—the experience of brokenness or division between body, mind and soul. The reason I said it leads to this is because I spoke about a struggle and tension. It seems to me that to be a Christian is to be in struggle, to be involved in an "unseen warfare," as one book which talks about spiritual life is so wisely called.

In the early Christian Church there were a number of conflicts which arose, such as Arianism and Nestorianism. These dealt with the person of Jesus Christ. There were questions raised whether He had two natures—divine and human—or just one. If He had two natures, was the one stronger than the other? It strikes me that in some ways these questions or issues are still lived out today in relation not to Christ but in regard to what it means to be a human being. We live in a physical world and are physical beings with a body and a mind. But to be human is more than that. We are also spiritual beings. We have the ability to relate with things beyond our own physical limits—to relate with things even beyond the limited realm of our own personal experience.

This is something that is taught both by theologians and by many psychologists, such as Carl Jung. As human beings made in the image and likeness of God, we can, although being part of the created, relate with our Creator. To be both physical and spiritual beings is to live with some tension between the two. It is to live in a process. As Christians, we live in a world where the Kingdom is here—but not yet manifest. We await the return of Christ to experience fully the presence of God.

We live in that process where we can experience the Holy Spirit as very close to us one day and so very far away another. To be in process is important both in regard to growth as a person and as a Christian. To be willing to live in the tension, to be willing to live between intimacy-closeness and absence-separation is very much part of our growth as fully human persons and as Christians.

We sin against ourselves, against the way we were created, when we do not recognize and respect the very high calling and high potential we have as human beings. We sin against ourselves when we allow ourselves to become only a body or mind or a soul without working toward wholeness and integration. Through the incarnation of Jesus Christ, we see both our oneness with all of humankind and with all of creation as well as our oneness with Him who made us.

It is very much part of Orthodox theology that life is sacramental, that we are to mark the presence of God in all creation, in all that we do. This is the work of all Christians and particularly of the priest. Our ministry should be incarnational. We are witness to the presence of God, to the presence of Christ in all of life. We are, through our own presence as representatives of the Body of Christ, to represent Christ, to make Christ present again.

At the same time, though, we are to enter into the pain, fear, anxiety and struggle of another person as a "wounded healer," in the way Henri Nouwen, former Professor of Pastoral Theology at Yale Divinity School, describes in his book by that name. When we enter into the brokenness and struggle of another person as wounded healers and truly listen, we recognize that the struggle they are dealing with is not just theirs but ours. As the psychologist Carl Rogers says in his book *On Becoming a Person*, "that which is most personal is most universal." We see and hear ourselves in that other person. Through that relationship, a sense of acceptance and community develop and healing takes place—not a healing neccessarily, but a healing that comes with this sense of wholeness and well-being.

I am reminded of the words of Jesus when He said, "He who has seen me has seen the Father" (John 14:9). I believe that when we enter in ministry into the experience of another and truly listen, we can see and hear ourself in that person. Only then can we respond to him or her with genuine sensitivity and care. When this is done in the name of Christ, with an openness to His presence, we also can see and hear Christ. The relationship becomes truly spiritual. The human person is truly physical, emotional and spiritual . . . and Glory be to God!

About the Editor

JOHN T. CHIRBAN, Ph.D., Th.D. is Chairman of the Department of Human Development and Director of the Office of Counseling and Guidance at Hellenic College at Hellenic College and Holy Cross School of Theology, Brookline, Massachusetts. He is an Associate in Human Development at Harvard University, and he also maintains a private practice in psychotherapy in Cambridge, Massachusetts.

Among Dr. Chirban's recent writings are "Developmental Stages in Eastern Orthodoxy"; *Transformations of Consciousness* (Kenneth Wilbur, New Science Library: Random House, 1986); *Thalassemia— An Interdisciplinary Approach* (Editor, University Press of America, 1986); *Youth and Sexuality* (Hellenic College Press, 1985); *Medicine, Psychology and Religion: New Directions, New Implications* (Editor, Holy Cross School of Theology, 1983); and *Human Growth and Faith: Intrinsic and Extrinsic Motivation in Human Development* (University Press of America, 1981).